SPIRITS, SOULS, *and* DREAMS

Poetic Impressions

ORDINARY IMMORTAL

abbott press

Abbott Press books may be ordered through booksellers or by contacting:

Abbott Press
1663 Liberty Drive
Bloomington, IN 47403
www.abbottpress.com
Phone: 1-866-697-5310

ISBN: 978-1-4582-1692-2 (sc)
ISBN: 978-1-4582-1693-9 (e)

Library of Congress Control Number: 2014910975

Printed in the United States of America.

Abbott Press rev. date: 07/14/2014

Ephesians 5:19

*Speaking to yourselves in psalms and hymns and spiritual songs,
singing and making melody in your heart to the Lord;*

CONTENTS

PREFACE

Before you is a collection of unique perceptions of myself and how I perceive others. The extremes of torment and bliss are now yours to experience; the boundaries of which have no border or limit.

INTRODUCTION

Spirits

The origin of life. The Bible purports that in life, *"we wrestle not against flesh and blood, but against principalities, against powers, against the rulers of the darkness of this world, against spiritual wickedness in high places"* Ephesians 6:12. Thusly, our spiritual perceptions are not exclusively from God, but also from The Devil, *"Beloved, believe not every spirit, but try the spirits whether they are of God: because many false prophets are gone out into the world"* 1 John 4:1.Various spiritual topics are broached herein such as: faith, expectation, reassurance, prayer, acceptance, questioning, foretold future, vigilance, awareness, thankfulnesss, guilt, wariness, cautiousness, hope, helplessness, appreciation, obgligation, courage, worship, and spiritual battle. In reality we are guided as well as misguided. We confront demonic principalities, and consequently we all are intimately acquainted with the dark forces of spirit according to the bible, whether we perceive this or do not.

Souls

One's intellect, will, and emotions and how one navigates through love, love's troubles, love lost, desperation, delusion, vulnerability, incomprehension, wonder, mortality, significance of time, misunderstanding, concern for others, disappointment, hope, expectations not met, altered awareness, acceptance of what is, exhortation, encouragement, questioning societal norms, dangers, fear, perseverance, loss of hope, selfishness, deception, thankfulnesss and trust. These are some of the issues encountered in the Soul sphere. The extent to which spiritual forces are expressed in the Soul plane may be characterized by the following. 1 Peter 5:8 *Be sober, be vigilant; because your adversary the devil, as a roaring lion, walketh about, seeking whom he may devour.*

Dreams

The convergence of spirituality and humanity, good and evil, reality and fantasy, fear and courage, thought and feeling. In dreams the supernatural, imigination, presumed reality, the past, present and future and all of our experiences are assimilated into both real and deceptive perceptions.

Daniel 2:19 *Then was the secret revealed unto Daniel in a night vision. Then Daniel blessed the God of heaven.*

Ecclesiastes 5:7 *For in the multitude of dreams and many words there are also divers vanities: but fear thou God.*

This collection of writings is based on the author's perceptions derived from Spirits, Souls and Dreams. The human experience entails living between spiritual heaven and hell, experiencing human emotions and thoughts with spiritually impaired reasoning, and subjectively interpreting singular and recurring dreams from both spiritual and human origin. Given these inherent convolutions, the author would like to exhort one invariable truth: as a human, it is quite easy to be mistaken. We are fallible in judgment and in our memories. Consequently, it is imperative to employ the utmost judiciousness to interpersonal inferences, assumptions and deductions; and with biblical conviction, accept that our cognitive processes are compromised.

It is absolutely essential to accept others without compromise. Acceptance is requisite for forgiveness. Forgiveness is indispensable for true love. God is love. Love is God.

CHAPTER 1

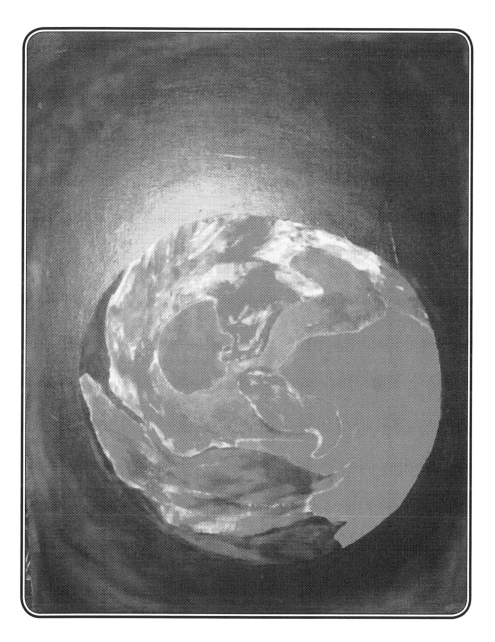

THE TUMBLING

The Tumbling Through The Sky
Alone In The Silent Night
Lost Our One Hope For The Earth
About Two Thousand Years Ago

You Look So Hard To Find
The Solution To Everything
You Know Now It Can't Be Found
In This World Of Deception

Still We Walk On
Right Into The Fire
Ready Or Not
The Outlook Is Dire

You Say You've Lost Your Mind
But Nobody Listens
Do You Think They Can Find
The Soul You Are Missing

We'll Never Live In Love
In This World Of Delusion
With Hands Tied And Dying
What A World Of Deception

Still We Walk On
Right Into The Fire
Ready Or Not
The Future Looks Dire

Do You Not Hear Our Cry
Did You Turn Your Face Away
When Will You Come Again
To This World Of Deception

HE DOESN'T SEE

He Had Enough Of The Things He Was Told To Like
He Had It Up To Here With Modern Life
He Wasn't Listening To Thoughts Of Other Men
He Couldn't Find The Heart They Stole From Him

He Goes Around The World
Upside Down
Trying To Find Meaning
Never Found
Doesn't Know He Needs
The King Of Kings
He Doesn't See

Away From Me He Said
I Don't Need This Conundrum
You Made Me Feel So Free
But How Do I Know The Road To Walk On

Why Can't I See You
You Said That You Would Always Be With Me
Can I Touch You
Any One Of You Three

He Goes Around The World
Upside Down
Trying To Find Meaning
Never Found
Doesn't Know He Needs
The King Of Kings
He Doesn't See

THE TIME IS NEAR

When Will I Wake Up
From This Dream
And Start My Real Life
With You

I Feel You Close
All Around Me
But I Still Miss You

Sing Out You Angels
The Time Is Near
River Of Life
Drink Of It Here

Let Your Kingdom Come

I'll Be With You There
In Heavens' Light
No More Despair
Out Of This Night

Let Your Will Be Done

When Will I Wake Up
From This Dream
And Start My Real Life
With You

I Feel You Close
All Around Me
But I Still Miss You

I'LL BE WITH YOU

I'll Be With You
Wherever You May Go
When You See
Darkness There I'll Be

When The Deep
Is Surrounding You
You Won't Sink
Cause I'll Be Holding You

I Can Hear The Lord's Voice From Heaven
Telling Us Don't Be Afraid
In The Times That Soon Must Come To Pass
I'll Be With You

Gotta Walk Through The Desert
To Get Back To The Garden
To Your Home
Help Those Whose Feet May Slip And Fall
Beside Your Own

When You Trust
You Will Discern
In The Fire
True Love
Does Not Burn

When You Hurt
The World Can Seem So Cruel
But If You Fall
I Will Carry You

I Can Hear The Lord's Voice From Heaven
Telling Us Don't Be Afraid
In The Times That Soon Must Come To Pass
I'll Be With You

Gotta Walk Through The Desert
To Get Back To The Garden
To Your Home
Help Those Whose Feet May Slip And Fall
Beside Your Own

WHO IS GOOD

Who Is Good
I Wonder Who
No Not You

No One
No One Is Good In This World

You Are Alone
When You Stand Before The King
And You Have To Hide Your Face
Cause His Light Is Penetrating Your Soul

Physician Who's Helping Whom
People Are More Than What You Do
Why Do You Act As Such A Fool

Leaders In The Capitals And Steeples
You Want To Own All Of The People
Would You Be Their Only King

Who Is Good
The One Who Loves
The One Who Puts Others Above

Who Is Good
I Wonder Who
No Not You

ON US ALL FALLS THE RAIN

You Tell Me
There Is No Answer
There Is No
Cause For The Pain

Maybe It's Time
You Look Up To The Heavens
You'll See That
Life's Not A Game

I Know What You're After
I've Been There Before
I Told You His Name
Go In The Narrow Door

He Already Loves You
People Need The Lord
To Show You The Way
He's The Only Way

Some People Walk In A Desert
Some People Live In A Daze
He Will Give You His Lifeblood
Why Do You Look So Amazed

You Know Faith Needs An Action
Let Your Love Light The Flame
Can't Live Your Life By Rehashing
On Us All Falls The Rain

I Know What You're After
I've Been There Before
I Told You His Name
Go In The Narrow Door

He Already Loves You
People Need The Lord
To Show You The Way
He's The Only Way

ARMAGEDDON

Nothing In This World Lasts Forever
Mountains Will Be Cast In The Ocean
Then Only The Wind Will Creep Over
Your Grave Your Heart Your Emotion

Armageddon
Armageddon
Armageddon

The Race Is Not To The Swift In Life
But Time Is Running Down Your Life
Jesus Gave The Gift To You Of Life
It's Not Too Late To Turn Yourself Around

His Heart Had Just One Intention
His Blood Spilled Out For The Offering
His Arms Nailed Out For His Children
His Life Given Up Till Armageddon

Armageddon
Armageddon
Armageddon

You'll Look For The Church Of The Light In The Night
But Time Is A Thief It Will Take Your Life
One Day It Will Be Too Late To Save Your Life
It Took The Blood Of An Innocent Man

Didn't Anyone Tell You
Nothing In Life Is Free
Will You Live Forever
Look At Your Family Tree
Jesus Gave Up His Blood For You
What Else Do You Want Him To Do

Armageddon
Armageddon
Armageddon
(Scream)
Never A Time To Remember
There's No Sun Underground
Everything You've Ever Thought Of
The Time That You Heard This Sound

SEVEN SPIRITS

Watch What You're Saying Now
Try To Leave It
Looks Like A Storm Is Brewing
No Time To Cover Up
I'll Be Searching From High Ground
The Night Is Long

On Through Time
Through This Place
Place Spirits Flying
Around You
Burning Faces And People
Jump Out Again

I Saw The Seven Spirits
Heading Right For You
I Went Straight Underground
I Tried To Look For You
I'll Be Searching From High Ground
The Night Is Long

On Through Time
Through This Place
Place Spirits Flying
Around You
I Don't Know Where To
Try To Find Your Soul Again

If You Can Hear Me Now
Don't Say Anything
Ears Are Listening
To Thoughts You're Thinking
I'll Be Searching From High Ground
The Night Is Long

I'm Gonna Walk To The Bottom Of Hell
Burn My Feet On Stones Of Fire
Won't Come Up For Air Without You
You Just Fight Until I Find You
I'll Be Searching From High Ground
The Night Is Long
I Don't Know How Find Your Screaming Soul

FROM THE SKY

Something Tells Me That I'm Never Gonna See You Again
Can Time Leave Us Lonely
Try To Remember I've Got Only One Human Life
No Time To Live Out All This Heartache And Strife

I'd Give Anything For You Just To Hear Me
I Can't Live On This Way
Why Did You Take My Heart If You Didn't Love Me
I Scream Out To The Sky Tonight

I'm Calling
I'm Holding On To You

Angel Why Are You Hiding
I Know You Can Hear Me
Tell Me Things From Heaven
Come Down Beside Me
Angel My Heart Is Crying
It's Breaking You Know Why
You See Me Where You're Flying
Come To Me From The Sky

If I Had One Wish Upon A Star
I'd Find Out Where You Are
I'd Travel On Starlight Just To Reach You
The World Would Spin Round For Me That Night

I'm Calling
I'm Holding On To You

Angel Why Are You Hiding
I Know You Can Hear Me
Tell Me Things From Heaven
Come Down Beside Me
Angel My Heart Is Crying
It's Breaking You Know Why
You See Me Where You're Flying
Come To Me From The Sky

FLYING ME TO ETERNITY

From The Moment I Met You
I Knew I Had Something
When I Finally Opened The Door
My Heart Started Jumping

I Could Feel Your Life In Me
Stirring In My Soul
My Heart Felt Like It Had Wings
Flying Me To Eternity

Flying Me To Eternity
Flying Me To Eternity
Flying Me To Eternity
Flying Me To Eternity

You Waited For Me
When I Said You Didn't Exist
What I Didn't Know Back Then
I Was Already In Your List

I Could Feel Your Life In Me
Stirring In My Soul
My Heart Felt Like It Had Wings
Flying Me To Eternity

Flying Me To Eternity
Flying Me To Eternity
Flying Me To Eternity
Flying Me To Eternity

WHAT HAVE YOU DONE TO THIS PLACE

You Were Taken From My Side
When I Woke Up And Opened My Eyes
You Were Leaning Above Me
Then We Both Had To Cry

Can You Hear My Breaking Heart Beat
It's Shaking Out Of Me
The Ocean Water Flows Deep
Swim In The Waves With Me

The Love We Seek Is Nearby
When We Know Our True Worth
We Can Just Watch Life's Years Fly
Or We Can Find Our Spirit Birth

Things Will Tear Us Away
From Who We Were Designed To Be
Point Your Foot Down Forward
Take This One Step With Me

Can You Hear My Breaking Heart Beat
It's Shaking Out Of Me
The Ocean Water Flows Deep
Swim In The Waves With Me

There's Someone Who
Walks On Top Of The Water
He Said Turn The Other Cheek
But Nothing Is Harder Than Loving One Another
We Value Proud Over Meek

And The Lion Came
And The World Was Cindering
And He Said To The Man And The Woman

What Have You Done To This Place

Can You Hear His Breaking Heart Beat
It's Shaking Out Of Him
The Ocean Water Flows Deep
Drown In The Waves Or Swim

TIRED OLD MAN

You're A Tired Old Man
I Don't Care What You Have To Say
I Don't Wanna Hear Your Plan
Get Out Of My Way

You Better Hide
Cause You Know You Can't Run
You Should Head For The Highway
But You Always Reach For Your Gun

Get Out Of Here
Time Will Bring You To Your Knees

You're A Tired Old Man
I Don't Care What You Have To Say
I Don't Wanna Hear Your Plan
Get Out Of My Way

You Don't Feel
What You're Supposed To
You Don't Love Other People
You're Opposed To
You Could Make Heaven
But You Choose Hell

Get Out Of Here
Time Will Bring You To Your Knees

You're A Tired Old Man
You Fell As A Light From The Sky
Craving Glory Was Your Sin
There's Only One Most High

You're A Tired Old Man

WHERE I BELONG

God Of Mercy God Of Grace
How Could I Look In Your Face

You Took Away My Sin
Blood From Heaven Washed Me In

I Can Walk On In
You Are My Family
I Can See Your Face
Smiling At Mine

I Can Be At Peace
There Are No Enemies
In This Place Of Love
Where I Belong

God Of Love Out In Space
Can You Show Me To That Place

I Can Only Turn My Head
From This World Of Hate And Death

I Can Walk On In
You Are My Family
I Can See Your Face
Smiling At Mine

I Can Be At Peace
There Are No Enemies
In This Place Of Love
Where I Belong

DESTROYER

I Make You Love All The Things In Life
That Money Buys
I Show You All The Ways To Win
Just Hide Your Eyes
You've Been Rolling Around All Night
From What You've Done
Too Late You Realize
There's No Where To Run

You Don't Believe In Me
But You Know Me
I Don't Need To Show You
Who I Am
I Don't Want You To See
I Am The Destroyer
Destroyer
I'm In Your Head
Telling You What To Think

It's So Easy To Fool The Proud
And The Greedy One
They Who Refuse To Believe The Truth
Make My Life Fun
And Misery Is The Fruit Of A Life
Lost Chasing Me
Look At All The Souls I've Used
Through History

You False Zealots Who Claim To Live
For The Lord
If You Do Your Good Work
For Some Reward
Has It Crossed Your Mind That

Your Sacrifice Is Just A Lie
If Love Is Not Your Quest
You See Through My Eye

You Don't Believe In Me
But You Know Me
I Don't Need To Show You
Who I Am
I Don't Want You To See
I Am The Destroyer
Destroyer
I'm In Your Head Telling You What To Think

YOU'VE GOT POWER

You Got My Attention
My Heart Is In Deep
My Mind's Of The Clatter
Of Frivolous Things
I Put Down The Elements
I Usually Seek
I Don't Trust The Logic
Of My Personality

But You've Got Power
And All That I Need Is
Available To Me
You Know Every Thought
And Everything We Do
And You Use Circumstances
To Bring Us Back To You

The Thoughts That Come
From My Brain
Make Me Think
There's No Hope For Me
My Humanness
Makes A Sad Travesty
Where Under Heaven
Can I Ever Find Peace
What My Heart Knows As Real
Is Far, Far From Me

But You've Got Power
And All That I Need Is
Available To Me
You Know Every Thought
And Everything We Do

And You Use Circumstances
To Bring Us Back To You

I Can Do Anything Through God Who Strengthens Me

I Can Do Everything Through God Who Strengthens Me

CHAPTER 2

IN A LONELY GARDEN

In A Lonely Garden
Where You Lost Your Innocence
I Could See All The Diamonds Glowing
Did You See Where Your Life
    Was Going

In The Dark You're Taken
Where You Gave Your Soul Away
Tell Me What Was Spoken
Tell Me What Did That
    Serpent Say

Eve
The Lord Told You
He Said
Please Heed My Truth
In This World Keep Your Eyes Wide Open
Someone Is After You

Your Face Looks Different
Your Eyes Release Drops Of Rain
You Bartered Your Life For Knowledge
That Only Will Bring You Pain

Into Dark You're Taken
But I Cannot Enter There
What Is Our Love If Now Forsaken
What Are Our Lives If Not To Share

Eve
Why Couldn't You See
He Said
Please Heed My Truth

What Is Done Is Done
I Can't Leave You
Give Me The Fruit
Forgive Us Lord
Please Save Our Children
Forgive Me Lord
Please Save Your Children
Forgive Us Lord
Please Save Us

SAY A PRAYER FOR ME

Somebody Help Me
See The Light
I've Got Nothing
That Feels Right
Light A Candle
For Me Tonight
All Is Dark
Within My Sight

Say A Prayer For Me
That I Can Stay Up On My Feet
Talk To God For Me
Clear My Head From This Deceit

I See A Stranger
When I Look In The Mirror
I'm Hunted Down
By The Things I Fear
My Head Is Hurting
My Body's Weak
Please Help Me Find
What I Seek

I Can't Ask
For These Things Myself
He Wouldn't Listen To
What I Say
My World, My Life
My Health
Were Lost On
The Wider Way

Say A Prayer For Me
That I Can Stay Up On My Feet
Talk To God For Me
Clear My Head From This Deceit

YOU LOVE US ANYWAY

You Created The Stars
All Around Me
You Gave Breath To
The Winds In The Sky
You Made Us In
Your Holy Image
Mothers Love
And Babies Cry

You Are The One
Who Lives Forever
Way Up High In The Clouds
You Look Down Upon The Day
You Call Us All To Sweet Surrender
You See All Of Our Sins
And You Love Us Anyway

You Direct The Way
Times Must Be Written
You Stand Up For The
Innocent And Meek
Kingdoms And Men Fall Down
In Your Wisdom
When You Say
Your Time Is Done

You Are The One
Who Lives Forever
Way Up High In The Clouds
You Look Down Upon The Day
You Call Us All To Sweet Surrender
You See All Of Our Sins
And You Love Us Anyway

YOUR BROTHER'S BLOOD

Why Do You Hide Yourself
From Me
As If You Could Run

Now Tell Me Where Is
Your Brother
What Have You Done

Your Brother's
Blood Cries Out From The Field
You're Cursed From The Earth
By Your Own Hand

The Ground Will Not Yield
Her Strength
You Will Sow
But Not Reap

You'll Find No
Home To Rest Your Feet
A Traveler You'll Always Be

Your Brother's
Blood Cries Out From The Field
You're Cursed From The Earth
By Your Own Hand

THE JUDGMENT OF THE ANGELS

Some Of The Angels Of Heaven
Did Transgress The Word Of God
Uniting Themselves With Women
Their Children Were Risen
With Chains Shall These Angels
Be Bound For Ever
In Their Place Of Destruction
They Will Be Imprisoned

Are You All Too Blind To See
The Judgment Of The Angels
Here On The Western Wall
Your Tears
Fall On Empty Ears
Your Prayer Sounds Don't Even Reach
The Gates Of Heaven

Bringing To Earth The Giants
Of Spirit, Flesh And Tears
There Will Be Great Retribution
On The World
Upon The Earth Shall Reside
The Spirits Who Are Born Here
Spirits Of The Wicked
Shall They Be Called

Before The Lord Of Spirits
Shall Be No Idle Word
The Lord Shall Judge
The Secret Things Of Your Life
None Shall Utter A Lying Word Before Him
Do Not Approach The Almighty
With Your Fool's Tongue
And Heart Of Hate

Are You All Too Blind To See
The Judgment Of The Angels
Here On The Western Wall
Your Tears
Fall On Empty Ears
Your Prayer Sounds Don't Even Reach
The Gates Of Heaven

WHAT ARE YOU DOING TO US

You Told Abraham Your Name
Mohammed Said
You Were Someone Else
Christians Believe That Jesus Came
We Can't Make Peace Among Ourselves

What Are You Doing To Us
What Have You Done To Us
What Are You Doing To Us
What Have You Done To Us

The Deceiver Fools The Many
Beyond Our Perception To Understand
I Guess Some Souls
Aren't Worth A Penny
The Way They
Vanish From Your Hand

What Are You Doing To Us
What Have You Done To Us
What Are You Doing To Us
What Have You Done To Us

Is This Some Kind Of Test
Where You Are Not Absolute
We Have To Do Our Very Best
To Love Others More Than Truth

What Are You Doing To Us
What Have You Done To Us
What Are You Doing To Us
What Have You Done To Us

YOU GAVE UP YOUR LIFE FOR ME

The Things You Said
I Could Not Believe
To Love My Enemy
Does Not Make Sense To Me

You Said You Gave Up
Your Life For Mine
To Get To Heaven But
I'm Not Even Trying

And I Don't Really See
Why You Gave Up
Your Life For Me
And I Don't Really See
Why You Gave Up
Your Life For Me

You Love Me Though I
Rant And Rave
You See Something
That I Don't Want To Save

I Told You Before That
I'm Not Worth Your Blood
You Open Your Arms
And Love Flows Like A Flood

And I Don't Really See
Why You Gave Up
Your Life For Me
And I Don't Really See
Why You Gave Up
Your Life For Me

YOU'RE SO COOL

You Are
Amazing
You're So Cool
You See All

You Are
Wonderful
You Contain The World
In Your Heart

You Spoke And The Sun
Turned From Dark To Light
You Started The Earth
Turning In Your Might
You Were Friends With
The First People That You Made
But We Had To Find Out If
We Would Stand Or Fade

You Are
Amazing
You're So Cool
You See All

You Are
Wonderful
You Contain The World
In Your Heart

You Breathed Your Holy Spirit
Right Into Man
Then We Tried To Control Things
And Lost The Land
But You Loved Us So Much
You Provided A Way
Now We're Back In Your Presence
We're Here To Stay

You Are Amazing
You're So Cool
You See All

You Are Wonderful
You Contain The World
In Your Heart

TEN

You'll Have No Gods Before Me
Nothing Can Represent Me
Don't Shame My Holy Name

These Ten Commands I Give To You
Love Each Other
As I Have Loved You

Keep My Sabbath Holy
Honor Your Mother And Father
You Know You Shall Not Murder
Be Faithful In Your Love

These Ten Commands I Give To You
Love Each Other As I Have Loved You

You May Never Steal
Tell No Lies
Speak The Truth
Don't Crave Another's
Anything
Love Others
As Yourself

These Ten Commands I Give To You
Love Each Other
As I Have Loved You

Love Me With
All Your Heart
Mind And Soul
Love Others
As Yourself

BRING ON YOUR HELL

Your Money
Is Of No Value
The Luck You Never Had
Is Repelled By You

Your Understanding
Is Diluted Away
By Stupid Things
You Hear People Say

Bring On Your Hell
Put Down Your Plowshare
A Time To Kill
Is Coming At You

You Wonder If This Happens
Only To You
And How This
Could Ever Even Occur
Shook To The Ground
By A Splinter Of Light
Finally Alive
Just Before You Die

Bring On Your Hell
Put Down Your Plowshare
A Time To Kill
Is Coming At You

Bring On Your Hell
Put Down Your Plowshare
A Time To Kill
Is Coming At You

IN THE SKY

A Wild Storm
In The Heart Of A Love
When One And One And One
Just Add Up To Two
You Don't Need To Find The Love Of Yet Another
Your Love Is At The Door Waiting For You

There's A Lull In The Sea Where There's Calm
And A Place In The Soul Where It's Free
In The Sky
We'll Dance And Hug Like Crazy
In The Sky
In Everlasting Love

Take This One To Be With The Lord And His Angels
And We'll Soon All Meet, There's An End To This
For A Short Time Now We'll Have A Heavy Heart
But In The Blink Of An Eye
We'll Have A Brand New Start

There's A Lull In The Sea Where There's Calm
And A Place In The Soul Where It's Free
In The Sky
We'll Dance And Hug Like Crazy
In The Sky
In Everlasting Love

Broken Hearts And People Dying
World War Seven Children Crying
People Walking Homeless Fleeing
Murder For A Diamond Ring

There's A Lull In The Sea Where There's Calm
And A Place In The Soul Where It's Free
In The Sky
We'll Dance And Hug Like Crazy
In The Sky
In Everlasting Love

God So Loved The World
He Gave His Only Begotten Son
That Whoever Believes
Would Not Die
But They Would Live Forever

WHEN THE CLOCK STRIKES TWICE

You Were A Light
You Talked To Him
You Were So High
Still Had To Sin

You
Did Not Listen
To The Voice
In The Sky
You'll Have To
Spin Easy
When The Clock
Strikes Twice

You Are The One
Who Planned
To Rebel
Now You Run
Away From Hell

You Had It Sweet
But For Your Pride
What Made You Think
You Could Usurp The Most High

You
Did Not Listen
To The Voice
In The Sky
You'll Have To
Spin Easy
When The Clock
Strikes Twice

JERUSALEM

Jerusalem
Jerusalem

Ishmael Says That
God Gave You To Them
Israel Says That
God Gave You To Them
They Both Follow You
They Both Follow You

David Bought You
From A Jebusite
Nebuchadnezzar
Took You In A Fight
Cyrus
Let The Jews Return To Town
Byzantines
Brought It Back Down

Jerusalem
Jerusalem

Romans Trampled It
All Around
Islam Took Over That Town
Crusaders Got It
But Not For Real
Israel Won It
But Didn't Close The Deal

If God Gave It To You
Let God Give It Back
If You Live By Faith
Let God Give It Back

City Of Peace
Where Isaac Almost Lost It
Jacob's Ladder
Shekinah On The Mount

Jerusalem
Jerusalem

YOU ARE LIKE A FIRE

You Are Like A Fire
Nobody Knows
Which Way You'll Turn
Warm And
Flowing On The Wind
Freeing Everything
Without Or Within

Won't You Start
A Fire In Me
You Can Use
This Field Of Weeds

You Are Like A River
That Flows
Over The Banks
Carrying The Burdens
Of People
Away From Their
Lives Of Pain

Won't You Flow
Your Waters Through Me
Take Me Out Into Sea

You Are Like A Fire
Nobody Knows
Which Way You'll Turn
Warm And
Flowing On The Wind
Freeing Everything
Without Or Within

Won't You Start
A Fire In Me
You Can Use
This Field Of Weeds

Won't You Start
A Fire In Me
You Can Use
This Field Of Weeds

OH HELL

Oh Hell
You Got
My Father

Oh Hell
You Took My Ma

I Cannot
Find My Daughter

Is She Smoking
In Your Hell

Oh Hell
You Stole My Sister

Oh Hell
That's All My Blood

A Wicked Bells
Tolls For My Wife

Could She Be
Under You Spell

Oh Hell
You're Waiting For Me

Oh Hell
I Can Tell

You've Got
Your Chains
On Me

Oh Lord
Can You
Set Me Free

CHAPTER 3

YOU MAKE IT HARD FOR ME

Holy Roller
Drug bag Holder
Cloud line Stroller
You Make It Hard For Me

Warlord Mister
Loan Arm Twister
Unfaithful Sister
You Make It Hard For Me

You Make It Hard For Me

At Midday
Night Has Fallen
What Is My Disease
It Feels Like A Thousand Degrees

Can't Change With The New Times
It's Hard To Pay For Your Crimes

For These Things I Fell
You Don't Care If I'm Going
        To Hell

Lonely Woman
Discarded Children
Execution
You Make It Hard For Me

Prostitutions
Old Solutions
Institutions
You Make It Hard For Me

You Make It Hard For Me

At Midday
Night Has Fallen
What Is My Disease
It Feels Like A Thousand Degrees

Can't Change With The New Times
It's Hard To Pay For Your Crimes

For These Things I Fell
You Don't Care If I'm Going To Hell

Hate Your Brother
Curse Your Mother
Go On A Killing Spree
You Make It Hard For Me

Your Blood Speaks To Me
Souls Meet Strongly
Death On Your Family Tree

You Make It Hard For Me
You Make It Hard For Me

YOU ARE THE ONE

You Are The One
Who Makes Me Open My Eyes
The One Inside
Who I Hear Whispering To Me

First Breath To Last
I Spend Sifting Through Sand
Living To Know You
But I Can't Cause I'm Just A Man

We Are Your Faithful Children
We Are Your Own Blood
We Are Your Revelation
Standing Here By Your Love
To As Many As Believed
You Gave The Right To Be Sons Of God
You Want Us To Follow You
The Storms Will Make Us Strong
To Learn What You Want Us To
We've Got To Step Out On Our Own
Jesus You Told Us
Our Faith Will Make Us Whole

You Hide Your Face From Me
You Reside In The Shadow
Until The Time You Please
This Life Will Be So Shallow

You Feel When My Heart Beats
But You Stop Me At Your Door
Why Do I Have To Plead
Just To Know You More

We Are Your Faithful Children
We Are Your Own Blood
We Are Your Revelation
Standing Here By Your Love
To As Many As Believed
You Gave The Right To Be Sons Of God
You Want Us To Follow You
The Storms Will Make Us Strong
To Learn What You Want Us To
We've Got To Step Out On Our Own
Jesus You Told Us
Our Faith Will Make Us Whole

LET HIS LOVE BEGIN

Hopeless Thoughts
Fill My Mind
Powerless
In This Endless Fight
I Struggle inside
Cause I Know That
I'm Not Right

Emotions Take Over
In My Head
I Walk In
The Devil's Den
Guts Me Out
Till I Wish I Were Dead
Tricked Into This Nightmare
Again

I Know
I Should Never Go There
Let His Love Begin
God Says Vengeance Is His
What Happens To Me, Happens To Him
To End Living In This Hell
I Need Is To Let His Love Begin

Terror Greets Me
Like A Best Friend
Silent Screams
From Deep With In
I Need To
Lash Out Again
In Despair And Broken
I Cave In

Not Enough Water
For All Of My Tears
My Heart Pounding Me
All Night
Then Your Word
Takes Way All My Fears
The Battle Is Yours
I Have No Reason To Fight

God Says Vengeance Is His
What Happens To Me, Happens To Him
To End Living In This Hell
I Need Is To Let His Love Begin

THE REAL YOU

What You See
And You Do NotSee
Make Up You

In The
Sky You See
In Eternal Color

Your Way
And All TheDays
In Tune
And You Harmonize
With Souls You Knew

In The Light You See
The Way To The One
Who Waits For You

YourArms
Out Turned
Your Hearts
Closing In
Love's Slow Burn

Wrap All Your Cares
And Throw Them Away
None Of Your Tears
Or Worries Can Stay

Wrap All Your Cares
And Throw Them Away
None Of Your Tears
Or Worries Can Stay

YOUR LOVE STAYS STRONG

Rapt In My Only
Thought That Meant Anything

And I Just Had To Leave
My Mind From Then On

In Deep Water I Call To You
You Hear Me
And Reach Out Your Hand

You See Me Falling
And You Keep Holding On
To My Unfaithful Life
Your Love Stays Strong

I Make No Sacrifice
I Just Try To Manage
I Know You Are, The Truth
But I Seek No Advantage
All Day I Fight Myself
And At Night There's Still More
You Help Me
Fight My War

You See Me Falling
And You Keep Holding On
To This Unfaithful Life
Your Love Stays Strong

Your Love
Stays
Strong

Your Love
Stays
Strong

Your Love
Stays
Strong

WOULD YOU CARRY ME IN

Oh Lord
I Hear You
Calling Me
FromThat Small
Voice Within

I Think I Know Now
How You Felt When You
Gave It All Up
For Our Sin

Would You
Carry Me In
Would You
Stop All The Running
And Take Me In
Would You Carry Me In
Would You
Look At My Heart
And Take Me In

Tear Drops Fall Down
Hit On My Feet
For All Who Do Not See

Just Like That Yosemite Waterfall
But It Can't Keep Up With Me

Would You
Carry Me In
Would You
Stop All The Running
And Take Me In

Would You Carry Me In
Would You
Look At My Heart
And Take Me In

GIVE ME SOME WATER

Give Me
Some Water

Because I Have
Great Thirst

Came From
A Dry Land

Where There
Is No Rest

Lord I Am Weary
Of The Pain

Give Me
Some Water

Living
Water

I Wait
Only For You

Till My
Time Is Through

Lord I Wait Only For You

GIVE ME THE BLOOD

I Think Somebody Is
Blocking Out My Light
I Don't Know Upon
Which Rock To Stand
I Can't Find The Path
By My Might
Again My Sin Clouds
The Great I Am

Dust To Dust
Is All I See
I Need Your Presence
To Guide Me
I Give Up The Sin
That Separates Me
Give Me The Blood
That Sets Us Free

Lord Keep Me On The Path
Lord Put Me On Track

I Was Fooled Into
Doing It My Way
I Was Tricked
By The Stealth Of A Trap
The Enemy Saw That
I Was Not Okay
The Enemy Knows
Just When To Attack

Dust To Dust
Is All I See
I Need Your Presence
To Guide Me
I Give Up The Sin
That Separates Me
Give Me The Blood
That Sets Us Free

Lord Keep Me On The Path
Lord Put Me On Track

Lord Keep Me On The Path
Lord Put Me On Track

GOD DOESN'T NEED

God Doesn't Need
Your Help
God Doesn't Need
This Song
But He Told Us To Love
So If You Want To Do
One Thing For Him

Love Your Enemy
Love Your Family
Treat Your Neighbor Right
Its Easy To Fight

God Doesn't Need
Your Help
God Doesn't Need
This Song
But He Told Us To Love
So If You Want To Do
One Thing For Him

Bring Them Water
Share Your Honesty
Be True To Your Mate
Its Easy To Hate

God Doesn't Need
Your Help
God Doesn't Need
This Song
But He Told Us To Love
So If You Want To Do
One Thing For Him

You Can Love
You Can Love
You Can Love

STAY IN MY HEART

The Words That You Said To Me
Make Me Think About
The Way Things Might Have Been
If I Truely Loved

Look At My Face
Do I Need To Say
Why My Human Love
Could Never Stay

You Know All The Reasons
For Things
That We Do
By Your Design
I Can't Hide From You
Stay In My Heart
Stay In My Heart

You Come In And Out
Of My Live Again
Lest I Forget
That You Are My Friend
Do You Hold Me Down
For Not Seeing Your Way
Just Tell Me Now
So I Don't Wonder Some Day

You Know All The Reasons
For Things
That We Do
By Your Design
I Can't Hide From You
Stay In My Heart
Stay In My Heart

Stay In My Heart
Stay In My Heart

ONLY CAN I LIVE TO SEE

Only Can I Live
To See
When The Moon
Turns Red
I Can Not Imagine
Dreaming In My Bed

I Want To Fly
Above The Sea
On A Brand New Morning
And Make Clouds
My Covering

For No Reason
It's Part Of Me

I Wanna Ride The Horses
That Go From Here To There
Walk On The Emerald Floor
And Slide On Up To You

I Want To Fly
Above The Sea
On A Brand New Morning
And Make Clouds
My Covering

For No Reason
It's Part Of Me

I Want To Fly
Above The Sea
On A Brand New Morning
And Make Clouds
My Covering

For No Reason
It's Part Of Me

AWAY IN A MANGER

And The Day Came Upon Me
That I Feared
Took Me At Midnight
I Put Back Your Ear

You Ask Me These Questions
Without A Right
Where Were You Hiding
When I Made The Light

Hang Me On A Cross
So Your Soul's Not Lost

Hang Me On A Cross
So Your Soul's Not Lost

Away In A Manger
He Came For Us
Shepards Did See
They Knelt In The Dust

He Came For Everyone
Angels Did Sing
He Came For Me
A Baby King

These Tears Have Fallen
Not For The Pain

All The Lost Children
Are Homeless Again

But My Love Is Stronger
Then What's Done In Haste
Dont Say Your Sorry
I See Your Face

Hang Me On A Cross
So Your Soul's Not Lost

Hang Me On A Cross
So Your Soul's Not Lost

Away In A Manger
He Came For Us
Shepards Did See
They Knelt In The Dust

He Came For Everyone
Angels Did Sing
He Came For Me
A Baby King

Hang Me On A Cross
So Your Soul's Not Lost

Hang Me On A Cross
So Your Soul's Not Lost

WHERE IS THE LIGHT

When Your Light Shines
Over My Life
I Can Feel Your Touch On Me

Your Love Drives Me
Like A Highway
Through A Path
On This Garden Street

Then You Hide
Where Is The Light
I Can't See
Darkness Encamps
Around Me

Where Is The Light
I Can't See
Darkness Encamps
Around Me

Where Is The Light

Then I Feel You Standing There
Then I See You Everywhere
There You Are Standing There
There You Are Everywhere

I'm In The Light
I'm In The Light

Floating
Along On The Waves
In The Palm
Of Your Hand
On The Sea
I Am Sailing
Searching For A Person
Who A Long Time Ago
Was Me

Then You Hide
Where Is The Light
I Can't See
Darkness Encamps Around Me

Where Is The Light
I Can't See
Darkness Encamps Around Me

Where Is The Light

Then I Feel You Standing There
Then I See You Everywhere
There You Are Standing There
There You Are Everywhere

I'm In The Light
I'm In The Light

It's Dark Now
I Look Around
But I See Only
Shadows Flee
A Strange Force
Pushes Right Through Me
To The Void
Where My Heart
Used To Be

Then You Hide
Where Is The Light
I Can't See
Darkness Encamps Around Me

Where Is The Light
I Can't See
Darkness Encamps Around Me

Where Is The Light

Then I Feel You Standing There
Then I See You Everywhere
There You Are Standing There
There You Are Everywhere

I'm In The Light
I'm In The Light

YAHWEH

Yahweh
Yahweh

Holy
God

You're So In Control
More Than We Can See
Each Breath We Take
All The Bodies In Space

You're In Everything
More Than We Ever Could
Imagine To Be
And You Are Our Father

Yahweh
Yahweh

You Love In A Way
Too High For Me
To Conceive
In A Day Of Eternity

Life Is A Journey
To Unfold The Mystery
That Calls Out To Us
Through Infinite Glory

Yahweh

Yahweh

THIS PATH BEFORE ME

If I Could Follow You
Life Would Be So Fine
Cause I Don't Know
Which Way To Turn
In This Hell Of Mine

You Said The Lame Will Walk
The Blind Will See
So Why Do I Fall On My Face
On This Path Before Me

You Give Me The Love
I'll Supply The Lame
You Give Me The Strength
I'll Bring The Pain
I'll Trade You Everything
I Thought Was Nice
For Your Presence In My Life

If I Could Look Up Above
I Would Be Better
Your Word Says I Am Loved
I Believe Your Letter

You Say The Lame Will Walk
The Blind Will See
So Why Do I Fall On My Face
On This Path Before Me

You Give Me The Love
I'll Supply The Lame
You Give Me The Strength
I'll Bring The Pain
I'll Trade You Everything
I Thought Was Nice
For Your Presence In My Life

CHAPTER 4

TAKE MY HEART

You've Got Pain
I Can See
If Your Feet Hurt
You Can Walk On Me
If Your Blood Can't Heal Your Ill
You Can Transfuse My Blood Till My Heart Is Still

Take My Eyes
If You Can't See
You Don't Need To Ask
Just Pull Them Out Of Me
Take My Spine
If You Can't Walk
You Can Take My Tongue And Lips
If You Can't Talk

Don't Want To See You
In Distress
You Can Have My Body
Put It To The Test
If It Will Make You Feel Alright
Please Take My Heart
My Breath My Might

Please Take These My Love
And Worry Not
It's My Joy To Give
To You All I've Got
I Would Trade My Life
Ten Times Until The End
Just To See You Happy
And Smiling Again

Take My Eyes
If You Can't See
You Don't Need To Ask
Just Pull Them Out Of Me
Take My Spine
If You Can't Walk
You Can Take My Tongue And Lips
If You Can't Talk

I HATE YOU

I Hate You
You Love Me

I Hate You
You Love Me

The First Time I Met You
I Gave You Some Of Me
You Felt A Strange Apparition
Then You Began To Bleed

I Hate You
You Love Me

You Never Lost A Thing
That I Didn't Take From You
You're Holding On
To What You Know Ain't True

I Hate You
You Love Me

You Say You Want Peace
You Say You Want Love
You Say You Believe
But All You Really Want Are Things

I Hate You
You Love Me

You're Deceived So Easily
You Chase After Me
For Things That You See
I Lead You To Them Because

I Hate You

NOW OR NEVER

Countless Suns Have Gone
The Way Of Darkened Energy
They Don't Have The Choice
To Burn Free
If You Look For Something
Out There As A Mystery
Look No Further
And Have Some Empathy

I Have Lived With All Creation
From The Ancient Times
This You Hear
But Cannot Comprehend
Trying To Grow You
And Trying To Know You
Until The Day
That I Can Call You Friend

I Have Seen So Many Of You
With Good Intentions Perish
And Also You
Who Did Not Love
So Few Of You
I Am Able To Renew And Cherish
So Very Few Who Climb Above

So Listen To These Words
Of This And Of All Other Time
From The One Who Stands Forever
I Invite You To My Heart
It's Still And So Sublime
You Have Just One Life
Its Now Or Never

FOUND MY LOVE

I've Heard Good News
I Changed My Fate
My Heart Feels So Free
Off My Shoulders
He Took The Weight
The Holy Spirit
Just Touched Me

I Just Found My Love Today
Things Must Be Going My Way
I Thank God For His Blessing
He Wouldn't Give Up His Love For Me

Did You Know He Died For You
His Ears Listen When You Speak
He Doesn't Hold You To Your Past
He's The First And He's The Last

I Just Found My Love Today
Things Must Be Going My Way
I Thank God For His Blessing
He Wouldn't Give Up His Love For Me

You Can't Buy Your Way To Heaven
You Can't Charge Your Soul With A Card
Only Blood Can Pay That Price
Don't Let Pride Steal Your Life

I Just Found My Love Today
Things Must Be Going My Way
I Thank God For His Blessing
He Wouldn't Give Up His Love For Me

YOU SEE PEOPLE

You See People
You Don't Recognize
In Your Head
When You Conceptualize
Pleading For Attention
In Your Life

You Are Under Spiral Medication
Don't You Wish You Had The Information
That Would Bring You Out From Behind The Door

Your Hair Blowing And Your Eyes Are Opening
You're Floating Higher As The Wind Sweeps You Away From
Where You Once Controlled The Waves From Crashing Over
Now You're Lost And Groping In This Timeless Stratosphere

And You Pray You Never Left The Ground
Faithful Courage You Have Never Found

Tic Tock Wakes You From A Strange Embrace
Nameless Lover With A Diamond Face
Does Not Shed A Tear When The Cutter Comes

Echo Music From A Sweet Guitar
Shadow Figure Playing From Afar
Twilight Hands Don't Even Touch The Strings

Your Hair Blowing And Your Eyes Are Opening
You're Floating Higher As The Wind Sweeps You Away From
Where You Once Controlled The Waves From Crashing Over
Now You're Lost And Groping In This Timeless Stratosphere

And You Pray You Never Left The Ground
Faithful Courage You Have Never Found

You See People
You Don't Recognize
In Your Head
When You Conceptualize
Pleading For Significance
In Your Life

You Are Under Abject Consternation
Don't You Wish You Had The Information
That Would Bring You Out From Behind The Door

WE ARE ALL ONE FAMILY

We Are All One Family
Trying To Make Our Way
With Lots Of Different Faces
And Things We Meant To Say

Not Everyone Gets A Funeral
Someone Has To Care
Not Everybody Has A Wedding
Some People Will Not Share

Some People Die Too Early
That Makes Us All Mourn
Some People Live Too Long
Some Are Never Born

We Are All One Family
Trying To Make Our Way
With Lots Of Different Faces
And Things We Meant To Say

Some People Hate Their Own Lives
Others Just Hang On
Some Wanna Rule Your Life
If You're Not Them You're Wrong

Some Hope To Reincarnate
They Chant And Meditate
Some People Cannot Find Peace
They Have To Medicate

Some People Work Till They Die
Others Sit And Beg
For Both Our Smiles Hide Disgust
But Hearts Are Not As Vague

We Are All One Family
Trying To Make Our Way
With Lots Of Different Faces
And Things We Meant To Say

YOUR LOVE

I, Evil
I, Spilled Your Blood
I, Shouted Curses
I Looked Up And Saw Your Face

Your Love Is Healing Me
Your Love Is Changing Me
Your Love Is Freeing Me
Your Love Is Guiding Me

You, Don't Remember
All The Times I Reject You
You Rather Love Me
Hold Me Close To You

Your Love Is Healing Me
Your Love Is Changing Me
Your Love Is Freeing Me
Your Love Is Saving Me

HUMAN SHELL

You're Caught In The Thoughts Of Your Human Shell
Closed Circle Potential
Break Out Of Your Living Hell
Leave The Past It's Broken

In The Dark Of The Night I See You
In The Dead Of The Night I Come To You
In The Heat Of Your Life I'll Comfort You

Do You Understand Me
I Need To Tell You
Gotta Use Your Power

You Blame Me
For Your Thought Slavery
As If It's I Who Bind You
It's You Who Holds The Lock And Key
Of Your Mental Prison

Free Yourself It's In Your Might
The Lives You Touch Are Waiting
The Stars Around Your Face Tonight
Leave The Sky Line Fading

In The Dark Of The Night I See You
In The Dead Of The Night I Come To You
In The Heat Of Your Life I'll Comfort You

Do You Understand Me
I Need To Tell You
Gotta Use Your Power

YOU AND I

You And I
We've Got Everything
I Can Always
Release Your Energy

And When I Get Repressed
You Know How To Bring Me Out
It's That Way With Everything
With You

I Got Every
Thing I Wanted To
I Took Home The First Prize
When I Found You

If I Were Stranded
Having Lost My Way
I Know That You Would Find Me
Walking The Other Way

You're The Only
One I've Ever Met
Who Could Spread Out
All Your Heart
And Catch Me
In The Net

You Know How To
Bring Me Out
It's That Way With everything
With You

I Got Every
Thing I Wanted To
I Took Home The First Prize
When I Found You

PROVE MY LOVE

I Know I Haven't Loved You
The Way That You Dreamed Of
But I Want Another
Chance To
Prove My Love
Prove My Love

I May Act Harshly
Before I Think
Please Forgive Me
Cause In A Blink
I'll Prove My Love
Prove My Love

I Always Loved You
You Know That
I Pray You'll Let Me
Have Another Chance

To Prove My love
Prove My Love

HUMAN CONVENTION

Triple Ambiguous
Incomprehension
We Are All Leaving This
Human Convention

Fusion Light Of Your Soul
You Pull Me Into The Glow
Since The First Time I Touched You
I Have Never Let Go

Wait For Me
On The Other Side
I'll Look For You
In The Sky
I Can't Help Myself
I Need You
I Can't Free Myself
I Need You
Gotta Have You
I Must Have You

Triple Ambiguous
Incomprehension
We Are All Leaving This
Worldly Convention

From The Land Of The Living
Pray The Lord Is Still Giving
Redemption For The Sinning
Or We're All Going Down

Wait For Me
On The Other Side
I'll Look For You In The Sky
I Can't Help Myself
I Need You
I Can't Free Myself
I Need You
Gotta Have You
I Gotta Have You

NOT WITHOUT YOU

I Don't Wanna Live
A Day Without You
I Don't Even Want To Try
You Make That
Leave Me Alone Look
The Poison Of Love I Took

Don't Leave Me Here
I Need You Now
Can't Detach From You
God Show Me How

Don't Leave Me Here Now
I Can't See
This Love Is Blind
It's Got To Me
You Stare At Me So Sadly
Got My Brain Spinning Madly
I Love You

You Stabbed My Heart
And Left Me Helpless
A Dark Sky
Without A Star
When You Walk Away
I Lose My Breath
Baby Don't You Run So Far

Don't Leave Me Here
I Need You Now
Can't Detach From You
God Show Me How

Don't Leave Me Here Now
I Can't See
This Love Is Blind
It's Got To Me
You Stare At Me So Sadly
Got My Brain Spinning Madly

I Don't Wanna Live My Life Without You
I Don't Wanna Live My Life Without You
I Don't Wanna Live My Life
Without You

YOU TURN AWAY

You Always Had All My Heart
These Days You Break It Apart
You Hate Me For Something To Do
I Still Can't Get Over You

And You Turn Away

I Don't Know A Night From The Day
I Need You To Light My Way
I've Got All The Wrong Questions
Your Life Is My Confession

And You Walk Away

God Gives The Earth To The Meek
Your Love Is All That I Seek
Ocean Waves Roll Over My Head
I Walked In Live Now I'm Dead

And You Swim Away

I Don't Know A Night From The Day
I Need You To Light My Way
I've Got All The Wrong Questions
Your Life Is My Confession

And You Turn Away

LOOKING AT YOUR SOUL

Looking At Your Soul
Reeling In Time Before You
Spirits That You Know
Springing Up For Expression

Now Your Light Kicks On
Freeing Up Your Face
Your Life Can Be Saved
When You Realize It's Grace

I See Your Thoughts In Waves
Gone With Just A Tear To Trace
We Stumble Through The Valleys
But We've Made It To This Place

The Pain That You Hold
Rising Up At This Moment
Long Trapped In Your Soul
Hard To Keep The Madness In Tow

Now Your Light Kicks On
Freeing Up Your Face
Your Life Can Be Saved
When You Realize It's Grace

In This Moment Time
Bridges Your Life To Eternity
Maybe We Can Find
The Tree Of Life Lost In Eden

PHONE LINE TO HEAVEN

If You Came As A Human
Would I Believe You
If You Bled For Me
Would I Bandage You

When You Said You Love Me
Was I Not Aware
When They Spiked Your Hands For Me
Did I Even Care

If I Had A Phone Line To Heaven
When Would I Call
You Warn Me About Every Trouble
Yet Still I Fall

You Gave Me Eternal Life
But I Don't Want To Leave
You Took The Sting From Death
Yet Still I Grieve
If I Had A Phone Line To Heaven
Would I Call

Your Life Ended Too Soon
I Know You Wanted To Stay
You Begged Me To Help You Through
But I Guess The Lord Had His Way

I Held Your Hand When You Left
So Uneasy
Then I Opened Up Your Eyes
Their Beauty Strengthens Me

If I Had A Phone line To Heaven
I Would Ask You How You've Been Doing
I'd Say Sorry For That Last Night
And I Really Miss You
If I Had A Phone line To Heaven
To Hear Your Sweet Voice Talking
If I Had A Phone line To Heaven
I Would Call You Just To Listen

CHAPTER 5

I DON'T NEED TO SEE YOUR WAY

In My Life
I Can Do What I Want I'm Free
In This Time
I Don't Need An Authority

When The Sun Settles
And All Is Done And Said
I'll Be The One Who Is Sleeping
In My Own Little Bed

I Don't Need To See Your Way
I'm Your Man
Listen To Me
I Just Want To Live My Life
Hold Your Criticism And Advice
I'm Your Man

If You Go On Speaking
To Change Me To Someone Else
Do You Feel The Sinking
You're Drowning My Real Self

When God Takes My Light Out
And I'm But A Memory
You Can Cry And Then Shout
There It Won't Bother Me

I Don't Need To See Your Way
I'm Your Man
Listen To Me
I Just Want To Live My Life
Hold Your Criticism And Advice
I'm Your Man

TELL ME WHAT MONEY CAN BUY

One Day You're In
One Day You're On
Around You Turn
And Then You're Gone

And Nothing That Money Can Buy

The Things You Learn
The Times You Laugh
Are Only Weeds
That Burn To Chaff

You Thought With Your Money You'd Last

Now It Ends
Now It's The Night
The River Bends
Turns Out Of Sight

Now Tell Me What Money Can Buy

LIVE YOUR LIFE NOW

Your Struggle Will End One Day You'll See
Sooner Than You Want It To Be
So Far Will You Be Out Of The Way
You'll Be Glad For The Trouble You've Got Today

Tracing Emotions Until They Collide
Biting My Nails I Feel Them Divide
Can't Find Any Mercy I'm Out Of Time
The Past Isn't Living So Why Do I Hide

Life Is Short Time Goes By Too Fast
Live Your Life Now Not In The Past
Even The Future Will Never Last
Live Your Life Now
Live Your Life Now

Your Time Will Be Over One Day
Sooner Than You Want It To
You'll Be Out Of The Loop All The Way
Enjoy What You Have Today

Put A Line On The Mirror Make It Cross Your Face
You May Not Like The Image It'll Be Replaced
Life Doesn't Wait You Know   If You're Not Satisfied
It Goes The Way All Things Go It's A One Ticket Ride

Life Is Short Time Goes By Too Fast
Live Your Life Now Not In The Past
Even The Future Will Never Last
Live Your Life Now
Live Your Life Now

FROM THE DARK OUTSIDE

You Can Take My Heart If You Want To
I Wouldn't Raise A Hand
I Hope This Love Is The Right One
But Will You Understand

Oh Oh Oh Oh Oh
Don't Turn Away
Without Seeing Me
Hey Hey Hey Hey Hey
This Is My Life
From The Dark Outside

Do You Know
I Wanna Be Your Man
Maybe This Time
In Every Soul's Plan

Oh Oh Oh Oh Oh
Don't Turn Away
See The Real Me
Hey Hey Hey Hey Hey
Can You Save Me
From The Dark Outside

In Love
I Never Seem To Find
The One Love
For The End Of Time

Oh Oh Oh Oh Oh
Don't Turn Away
Without Holding Me
Hey Hey Hey Hey Hey

Can You See Me
From The Dark Outside

Your Love Is
Like Life I Guess
Beyond My Reach
Now I Confess

Oh Oh Oh Oh Oh
Don't Turn Away
Without Loving Me
Hey Hey Hey Hey Hey
Can You Save Me
From The Dark Outside

PLEASE BE MINE

Please Be Mine
I Want To Hold You
Till You Are Breathless
Till The End Of Time

I Am Under
Your Sweet Love Spell
That You Made In The Clouds
From Which You Fell

In The Night
How Sweet Are My Dreams Of You
And The Day
Wakes Only For You

Now Think About This
And Say You Love Me
So I Don't Have To Beg God
Through Eternity

Please Be Mine
Please Be Mine
Please

DON'T LISTEN

Don't Listen
Don't Listen

You Don't Like To Know The Truth
You Don't Want To Know The Truth
You Will Feel Threatened

And Then You Will Defend Yourself
From Your Cocoon
Made In Self Deception

Don't Listen
Don't Listen
To These Words That Contend For Your Attention
They're Always Before You

Evil Is The Good
In Your Reverse Dimension
Of Eternal Suspension

Don't Listen
Don't Listen

Please Just Continue In Your Fear Of Truth
That Keeps You From Emerging

Yeah Keep Yourself Hidden In That Cloudy Murk
It's So Easy

Don't Listen
Don't Listen
You Are Not Alone Now
You Are In The Field Now
With Thoughts That Are Like Bullets
And Bombs Are Bursting In Your Head
Don't Listen
Don't Listen

DON'T HOLD YOUR LOVE

What Are You Doing
Today
The Night Is All Gone
You Can See Your Way Now

Don't Hold Back
Be Who You Really Are Now
You're Intact
You've Got Something To Give

Give Yourself Away
Don't Keep It
Somebody Needs You
Don't Hold Your Love In
You've Got To Use It

Don't Think What You Could Have Done
Do It Now
Waiting Is A Game
That You Don't Want To Play

Just Move Out
Don't Wait For A Sign
Times Moving On
You'll Never Catch Up

Give Yourself Away
Don't Keep It
Somebody Needs You
Don't Hold Your Love In
You've Got To Use It

EVERYBODY

I Can Tell By Your Heart
Your Face Is Heavy
You're An Ocean
Tossing A Way
You've Got To Let Your Life Be
A Blissful Highway

You Got Lost When You Pretended
Drop The Fake Tragedy
You Were Born To Live Suspended
On A Force That You Can't See

Everybody
Everybody
Everybody
Everybody
Everybody
Everybody
Love Everybody

Everybody
Everybody
Everybody
Everybody
Everybody
Everybody
Love Everybody

You Can Miss All The Life In Living
You Can Cover Up Your Light
You Can Add To The Chaos
Or You Can Put Up A Fight

It Doesn't Take That Long To Remember
When You First Believed The Lie
That Keeps You From Getting Over
You Should Be Flying High

Everybody
Everybody
Everybody
Everybody
Everybody
Everybody
Love Everybody

Everybody
Everybody
Everybody
Everybody
Everybody
Everybody
Love Everybody

SHOW ME YOU'RE DIFFERENT

Round And Round
The Sun We Go
Seasons Turn Away
Generations Melt Like Snow
We Won't Get To Stay

Hope And Love And Misery
Are The Same To You
Fortunes Won Flow To The Sea
Still We Fight To Lose

Show Me You're Different
Tell Me I'm A Liar
Show Me You're Different
Tell Me I Don't Know
Tell Me

Babies Born Only To Wither
As The Grass In Vain
Proud And Strong So Soon To Winter
Welcome To The Pain

We Ride On This Cosmic Wheel
Foreseeing Our Own Doom
All The Billions You Can Steal
Won't Slow Your Ride To The Tomb

Show Me You're Different
Tell Me I'm A Liar
Show Me You're Different
Tell Me I Don't Know
Tell Me

LOOKING OUT MY WINDOW

Looking Out My Window
Strangers Staring In
Horrible Faces
And Circus Skin

And I Woke Up
And Rubbed My Eyes
And Fear My Thoughts
And Look Outside

Looking Out My Window
Vehicles In Space
Counting Backward To Oblivion
Condemn The Human Race

Looking Out My Window
Flashing In The Sky
Watching All Your Children
Melt Before They Fly

Looking Out My Window
Looking Out My Window
Looking Out My Window

YOU ARE FREE

You Need Water
But You Curse The Rain
You Want Love
But You Can't Stand Pain
You Had A Vision
You Know What You Have To Be
Your Friend Confusion
Has Blinded All You See

Don't You Know You're Free
You Wonder If There's More To Life Then Ending
Look Through Yourself And See
Feel Your Soul Floating In The Clouds Ascending

Your Monkey
Is The Size Of King Kong
He Pulls You Back
From Where You Belong
You Can't Stand Up
Although The Waters Shallow
Drowning Till You Come Out
Behind Your Shadow

Accept Yourself
There's Nothing You Have Got To Live Up To
Perfection Is Just The Way You Are Designed
Your Monster Is Made Up In Your Mind

What You Think
Can Make You Love Or Hate
You Choose To Despair Or Appreciate
Do You Feel All Blocked In
You Can Leave All Of Your Troubles Behind

Don't You Know You're Free
You Wonder If There's More To Life Then Ending
Look Through Yourself And See
Feel Your Soul Floating In The Clouds Ascending

CINDERELLA

I Met Your Sisters
Along My Way
They Told Me You Can't
Come Out Today
You've Got Work
That You Have To Do
I Can't Wait
Till It's All Through

Cinderella
Cinderella Come To Me
I Don't Care If Your Hair Is Not Clean
Cinderella Come To Me
I'll Shake The Dirt
From Your Well Worn Sleeves
Cinderella Come To Me
Take Off Your Dress
Under These Trees

Your Beauty
Shines Out Through
Ashes From Your Face
I'll Move
Your Scraped Hands
Get No Rest
Feel Like Silk
On My Chest

Cinderella
Cinderella Come To Me
I Don't Care If Your Hair Is Not Clean
Cinderella Come To Me

I'll Shake The Dirt
From Your Well Worn Sleeves
Cinderella Come To Me
Take Off Your Dress
Under These Trees

Cinderella
Cinderella

DISCONNECTED

Take The Plaster Off Of Me
When Can I Ever Finally See
The Person You Designed
Maladjusted Much Maligned

Disconnected From My Life
Disconnected

You Said I Should See Forever
Living Here Is A Big Endeavor
Make The Clouds All Clear Away
Make The Sun Glow On The Day

Disconnected You And I
Disconnected

You Gave Me Adult A.D.D.
Biological Slavery
Cigarettes Attacking Me
My Friends Are From The Penitentiary

Disconnected From My Mind
Disconnected

Live My Life In A Black Hole
They Kicked Me Out Of Mexico
Relationships Are Lost At Sea
Love's A Distant Memory

Disconnected From My Life
Disconnected You And I
Disconnected From My Mind
Disconnected

ADDICTION

You're A Liar
And A Thief
You Make Excuses
Beyond Belief

Addiction
You've Got A Hold On Me
Addiction
Where Is The Road To Be Free

You Make Me Tired
And Anger
Is Not Far Away
I Don't Want To
See My Friends
Unless They
Enable Me Today

Addiction
You've Got Your Fangs In Me
Addiction
Where Is The Road To Get Free

Addiction At The Pharmacy
Addiction In My Body
Addiction In My Head
Addiction Into My Bed
Addiction In My Vein
Addiction Is Beyond This Plane Of Me

I'm Looking
For That Road
And I Have To
Find It
Don't Lead Me
To My Death
The Lord
Had To Buy It

Lord Save Me
From That Tall Shadow
Of My Addiction
Oh My Addiction

THESE ARE THE WORDS

Crazy
Stupid
Hatred
Hypocrisy

These Are The Words You Use To Describe Me
The Last Thing I Want Is To Disturb You
If You Could Change One Thing About Us
It Would Be Me

Envy
Negative
Jealousy
Obsessive

You Told Me That You Had Spring Fever
In The Middle Of The Month Of September
Why Would You Ever Do That To Me
You Tell Me Not To Judge Or Remember

Meanness
Cruelty
Unforgiving
Annoying

You Can Call Me What You Want To
I Can See Through Your Deception
But How Could You Wish Bad Upon Me
When All I Want From You Is Attention

Demeaning
Sarcastic
Hurtful
Arrogant

These Are The Words That I Thing Best Describe

You

CHAPTER 6

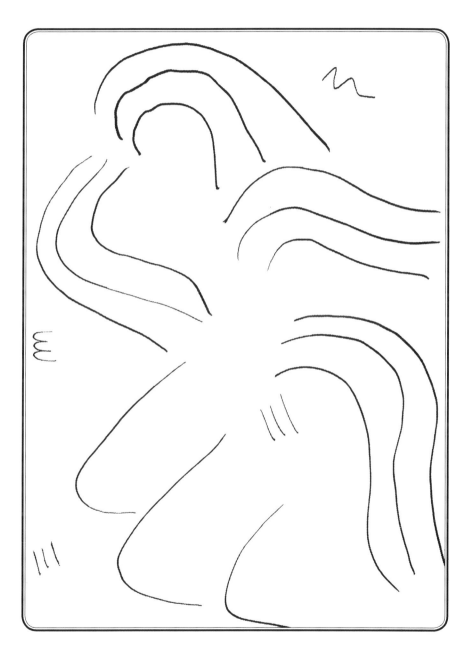

THIS SONG MEANS I LOVE YOU

You Cut Right Through My Serenity
You Look Up From The Table
I See Your Please Help Me Eyes
But I Am Not Able

Already I See That You're Broken
There's No Fight In You
Sometime Things Just Get Left Unspoken
But This Song Means I Love You

There's A Voice That's Close To Your Ear
If You Want You Can Listen

In The Morning It's Loud And So Clear
In The Night It's Still Ringing

Already I See That You're Broken
There's No Fight In You
Something Things Just Get Left Unspoken
But This Song Means I Love You

You Can Tell Right Now
I Wouldn't Fool You
But I Can't Show You How
In This Moment Near You

Already I See That You're Broken
There's No Fight In You
Something Things Just Get Left Unspoken
But This Song Means I Love You

IF YOU LOVED ME TOO

You Took A Ride On Our Wedding Day
You Never Felt Like You Could Stay
Do You Have The Time To Wallow Away
You Don't Realize There's Hell To Pay

Well I Cannot Delude Myself
I'm Lost From The Start Without Your Help
And You Would Not Even Tell Me That
I Was The Reason That You Came Back

I Look Around But Don't See Your Purse
Your Back Is Bad But Your Front Is Worse
But Why Do I Say These Things To You
You Act Like This Is Something New

Well I Cannot Delude Myself
I'm Lost From The Start Without Your Help
And You Would Not Even Tell Me That
I Was The Reason That You Came Back

Alone Is My Friend Alone Is Free
But Alone And Free Is Not How I Want To Be
If I Could Just Make It Clear To You
It Would Be My Heaven If You Loved Me Too

Well I Cannot Delude Myself
I'm Lost From The Start Without Your Help
And You Would Not Even Tell Me That
I Was The Reason That You Came Back

Alone Is My Friend
Alone Is Free
But Alone And Free
Is Not How I Want To Be
If I Could Just Make It Clear To You
It Would Be My Heaven
If You Loved Me Too
It Would Be My Heaven
If You Loved Me Too

THERE WAS A TIME

There Was A Time
When Your Eyes Were Open
There Was Only One Then
And No Weight Upon You

You Are Something
In This World
At Times I Feel
You Live
All These Lives In Time
But I Live In
Black Steel

There Was A Time
With No Past Nor Future
And Only Cold
To Bide The Time

Without Conversation
And No One
To Tell How You Feel
It's Not Good
To Be Alone

You Are Something
In This World
At Times I Feel
You Live
All These Lives In Time
But I Live In
Black Steel

YOU WOULDN'T KNOW

You Were In The Front
I Could Hardly See
I Didn't Know You Then

I Tried To See Your Eyes
Then You Turned My Way
I Would Never Be The Same

I Walked Up To You
Feeling Like A Fool
You Reached Out Your Hand
I Said You're Beautiful
You Told Me I Was Too
We've Been One Since Then

You Wouldn't Know
Everything You've Been To Me
I Can't Measure
The Love You Gave Me
Your Love Is Easy
And Your Heart Is True
I Can't Number
The Times You've Saved Me

One Look In Your Eyes
One Word From Your Lips
Makes Me Feel Alive
Your Love Makes Me Strong
No Need To Drive The Mainline
Just A Shot Of Your Love

You Wouldn't Know
Everything You've Been To Me
I Can't Measure
The Love You Gave Me
Your Love Is Easy
And Your Heart Is True
I Can't Number
The Times You've Saved Me

A VISION

You Appear
With A Smile To Me
Stop My Impropriety
I Revel In The Glow
So Sweet
I Don't Want To Know

You're Only Here In This Vision
Then You Fade A Way

I Cannot Help But Stare
You Are
Completely Unaware
Inside I Scream
But Do Not Speak
It's Not Destined
That We Meet

I Just Adore You For This Moment
Never To Again

Sometimes You Are
Here With Me
Heart Is Empty
Soul Is Free
You Don't Like
Odd Company
Of The World
That Burdens Me

You Came To Me
From Forever
Say You'll Never Leave

THE HANDS OF TIME FALL DOWN

Listen
All You People
From All Your Nations
Can You Hear
The Final Invasion

The Hands Of Time
Fall Down
We Cease To Worry
About Useless Things
When Bodies
Are In The Ground

Look Out
Christian People
Jew And Islam
Can You See
The Final Invasion

The Hands Of Time
Fall Down
We Cease To Worry
About Useless Things
When Bodies
Are In The Ground

The Hands Of Time Fall Down
The Hands Of Time Fall Down

The Hands Of Time Fall Down

N 14TH ST.

You Are The Unknown Astronaut
Who Lives In My Canteen
You Come Out
When I Drink
You Traveled A Billion Nautical Miles
To See What I've Been Doing
I Keep You In Our Garage

Green Light From
The Closet Ghosts
Who Want To Take My Soul
They Come Out In The Night
Footsteps Across The Floor
Wake Me Up
But No One Do I See
Blankets Cover My Head

Mr. Laparre Sells Us
Penny Candies From His Store
Our Milk Money Is Gone
No Time To Greet The Old Man
With His Monkey On The Chair
My Teacher Fell And Barfed

Cia Tries To Kiss Our Faces
As Rain Falls In Metal Tubs
She Stinks Like Rancid Oil
Yugo Neighbors
With The Pink Poodle
Take Me To Sunset Beach
My Towel Is A Cape

THE WORLD IS WRONG

Winter Wind
Calls Out Your Name
Leaves Me
Staring At My Door
Hard To Realize
You Won't Be Back To
Touch My Face

And The World Is Wrong
As Far As I Can See
For Taking What Was Mine
And Stealing It From Me
I Wait In Pain Forever
My Heart Is Crying Do Not Sever
Me

Every Winter I'm Susceptible
To Haunting From Your Soul
Where Time Is Imperceptible
And Still You Won't Let Go

Well My Troubled Up Heart Is Dying
Excuse Me For
Not Denying
That I Can't Live My Life
When You Are Gone
Please Help Me Get Along

The World Is Wrong
As Far As I Can See
For Taking Mine
And Stealing It From Me
I Wait In Pain Forever
My Heart Is Crying Do Not Sever
Me

GOTTA LIVE MY LIFE

You Put A Hole In My Heart
Blood Came Pouring Down
I Was Shaken For A Long Time
Until I Realized
The Game Was Over

Gotta Live My Life
I Can't Wait For Perfection
The Sun
May Not Come Out Tomorrow
I Can Shed My Tears
For All Eternity
But Love Hides Away
From The Self Absorbed

Sirous Got Killed Saturday On 680
His Family Keeps The Pain
Four Cars Crashed
And Everybody Cried
And The Road Was Cleared By Nine
Game Over

I Try So Hard
To Be Kind To You
Looks Like I'll Never Be
Who You Wanted
Just A Lost Cause
Of This World's Order
Until The Lights Go Out
And This Game Is Over

Gotta Live My Life
I Can't Wait For Perfection
The Sun
May Not Come Out Tomorrow
I Can Shed My Tears
For All Eternity
But Love Hides Away
From The Self Absorbed

YOU ARE CREATED FOR LOVE

You Are
Created For Love

You Are
Created For Love

Even When Your
Path Is Not Straight
Always If
Your Heart Feels Hate
In A Kind
And Loving Way
Show Somebody
Love Today
They're Not To Blame
Love Is A Healing Flame
Love Is Sweet

You Are
Created For Love

You Are
Created For Love

In The Hidden Person
Of Your Heart
With A Gentle
Quiet Remark
Understanding
Her Weaknesses
Honor Her Grace
And Humble Spirit
No Evil For Evil
No Insult For Insult
Give Her Love

You Are
Created For Love

You Are
Created For Love

You Are Created For Love

LOSE CONTROL

I Can See
You're Gonna Lose Control
Touch Your Switches
Like A Radio
Tune Your Channels
Till You Come In Clear
Raise The Volume
Baby In Your Ear

You And I Could
Win A Dance Contest
Shake Your Body
There's No Time For Rest
Rock You Up
And Then I'll Roll You Down
Hold You Tight
So You Don't Leave The Ground

You Can Be The Star
In My Movie
About Two Lovers
Who Are Lost At Sea
I'll Navigate You
From Beginning To End
Around The World
And I'll Come Back Again

I STILL HOLD ON

You Came
From My Body
In Joy I Felt
The Love Inside
And When
You Learned To Walk
I Was There To
Hold You Up
You Spoke To
Call On Me
And Every Word
You Said I Heard

I Still Hold On To Them
I Still Hold On
Now I Hold On

You Took A
One-Way Trip
But You Did Not
Tell Me Goodbye
When I Wonder
About You
I Have To Break
Into My Heart
If You Can
Think About Us
Remember
I Once Dried Your Tears

But You Can't Dry Mine
You Can't Dry My Tears
No One Can Dry My Tears

IS THERE ANYBODY I CAN BELIEVE IN

Is There Anybody I Can Believe In
Where Are The People With Love In Their Eyes
Got No Will To Live My Life In
A World Where The Future Cries

Do You Know I've Been Here Waiting For You
I've Got My Arms Wide Open
I Want Good For You And Not Destruction
I Want To Love You Let Me Take You In

You Don't Even Know The Life Planned For You
Open Up Your Eyes And See The Sun
Your Future Is Trying To Call You
Don't Answer It With A Gun

You Feel Captive But Your World Will Change
You Think Nobody Can Free You
Don't Believe Lies The Demons Exclaim
There's So Much You Have To Do

Haven't Got What You Would Call A Family
Got Nobody To Defend Me
Too Many Times I've Walked This Lonely City
I'm Gonna Pack My Head With Lead I Think

Don't Look At Me I Know I'm Not Wonderful
Don't Stare At Me I'm Nothing
Don't Waste Your Time I'll Be On My Way
All I See Is The Dark Of Day

Do You I've Been Here Waiting For You
I've Got My Arms Wide Open
I Want Good For You And Not Destruction
I Wanna Love You Let Me Take You In

You Don't Even Know The Life Planned For You
Open Up Your Eyes And See The Son
Your Future Is Trying To Call You
Don't Answer It With A Gun

You Feel Captive But Your World Will Change
You Think Nobody Can Free You
Don't Believe Lies The Demons Exclaim
There's So Much You Gotta Do

INTO THE MAZE

Woman
Where Are You Going Now
Woman
Where Are You Going Now

You're
Alone Now
Thinking Your
Uncaged

Now You're
Out Into The Maze

Woman
Why Are You Calling Me
Woman
Why Are You Calling Me

I'm Unlisted
But You Got Me
In Lock Phase

Don't Bring Me
Into Your Maze

I Told You
In Your Face
I Told You
In Your Face

You Don't Listen
You're In A Daze

You Need Faith
To Walk Through This Maze

TIANANMEN (HEAVENLY PEACE) SQUARE

For A Chance
Of Freedom
They Gave Their Lives

To Tell Their View
Young Students
Were Attacked By Tanks

In The Courtroom
They Stood In Line Quietly
Respectfully

For Others They Gave Themselves
They Knew Their Penalty Was Death
They Accepted Their Sacrifice

The Predetermined Verdict Was Read
They Walked Out Peacefully
Some Bravely Weeped
They Stood For Freedom
For A Chance Of Freedom

CHAPTER 7

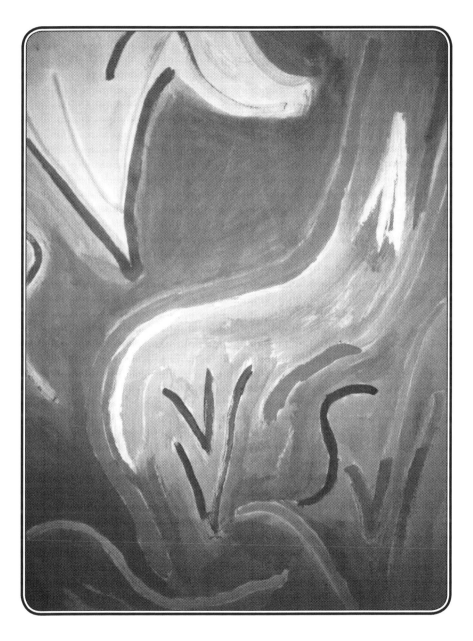

DISTRAUGHT GOODBYE

The Aircraft Detaches From The Jetway
You Are Torn From Me
My Existence Is Severed
My Life Descends

As The Plane Lifts Off
My Blood Is Poured
Into The Sky
Please Stop, You Are My Life

Clouds Obscure My Final Fleeting Bond With You
My Frail Heart Is That Of A Dying Man
Beating Weaker And Slower Until
Motionless

As You Proceed And Then Vanish
My Life Also Is Dissolved
In Scant Seconds Of Time
I Am Horrifyingly Altered

Walking Through The Terminal
People Speak,
ButI Hear Only Silence
I Am Alone
Devastatingly Wounded

What Would Occur Hereafter
Is Of No Consequence
To The Anguished Mind And
Fragmented Emotions Of This Soul

Driving Home
The Screams Of Silence From Emptied Seats
Echo Off Windows In Shrieking
Harassment Of My Trembling Tormented Being

At Home, The Sunflower Seed On The Floor
That I Complained About Yesterday
Now Quakes Misery In My Now Distraught Heart
To Recall The Sweet One Who Dropped It

Looking Upon The Couch
You Straightened For Me One Last Time
Is Now Torturous
Love And Life Have Forsaken Me
And Lay Bare Desolation

YESTERDAY I WANT TO SAY I LOVE YOU

You Did Not Tell Me 20 Years Was A Lifetime
Way Less Than I Could See
I Need To Fly Where You're Sleeping
Lay My Head Where You're Sweetly Breathing

Yesterday I Want To Say I Love You
Cause You Can't Hear Me Today
Yesterday I Want To Say I Love You
It's Too Late To Tell You Today

Time Won't Listen To Me
Time Won't Listen

God Can I Hold Her Again
Feel Her Face Touching Mine
In This Blackness, I Confide
I Can't Understand This Life

Yesterday I Want To Say I Love You
Cause You Can't Hear Me Today
Yesterday I Want To Say I Love You
Way Too Late To Tell You Today

You Did Not Tell Me Your Life Was A Lifetime
I Don't Have To Believe
I Wanna Fly To Where You Lie Sleeping
Lay My Face Where You Sweetly Breathe

Yesterday I Want To Say I Love You
You Can't Hear Me Today
Yesterday I Want To Say I Love You
But I'm Captured In Today

Time Won't Listen To Me
Time Won't Listen

God Let Me Hold Her Agatn
With Her Head Touching Mine
In This Blackness, I Can't Find
A Path To Chase Her Gleam Of Light

Yesterday I Want To Say I Love You

YOUR HEART TOLD YOU

Your Brothers' Blood
Drops On The Ground
But You Wont Slip On It
You Walk The Long
Way Around
The Struggle Is Over

The Tears Of Their Loved
Don't Make A Sound
In The Dirt
Of The Graveyard
Your Life Has
Progressed Way Too Far
To Worry About Their Feelings

The Day Turns
Around Into Night
And The Years
Turn Into A Lifetime
But What Is
Your Life Anyway
You See
A Blood Red Skyline

Don't Say
You Didn't Know
Cause Your Heart
Told You
The Choice Was
Before You
You Walked
Against Your Path
You Changed
Your Life
Your Hatred
Owns You
But Your Heart
Told You
Whose Blood
Is In The Path
Your Heart Told You

SELFISHNESS

If I'm Mean To You
It's Only Because
I Am Lost Myself
In Selfishness

If I'm Rude To You
I Feel Hurt Myself'
Then I Want To Die
In Selfishness

We Act
As If We Care
To Fake This World
Till Our Delusion Shatters
But In Reality
If We Dare
There Is Only One
Who Matters

In Our Selfishness

If I Reject You
It's Because I Can't Stand Me
But Myself I'll Not Condemn
So I Choose You

In My Selfishness
I Am Not Alone
You Are Just Like Me
In Selfishness

ILUSION OF CONTROL

Come On Out
Come On Out Of Submission
Your Thoughts
Are A Simple
Tool For Reason

Come On Out
Come Out Of Your Thought Prison
Say Goodbye
To Those Who
Dark Your Vision

Don't Try To Argue
You Might Believe Yourself
Keep Moving Higher
Don't Stumble On
The Illusion Of Control

You've Got Existence
Don't Wait Until The End
There Is No Distance
Believe Your Heart Again

There Is No Reward
For Pleasing Blood And Flesh
Look Up To The Skies
Forget Your Humaness

Don't Try To Argue
You Might Believe Yourself
Keep Moving Higher
Don't Stumble On
The Illusion Of Control

The Illusion Of Control

The Illusion Of Control

YOU MAKE ME LOVE MY LIFE

You're Lookin So
Pretty
In The
Moonlight

And I'll Tell You
One Thing
You Really Make The
Dark Bright

You Make Me
Love My Life

You Make Me
Love My Life

Just A Drop Of Your Rain
Can Fill My Ocean
The Mention Of Your Name
Stirs My Emotion

You Make Me
Love My Life

You Make Me
Love My Life

My Heart Is On It's Way
There's No Returning
You Bought It With A Smile
It's Yours For Certain

You Make Me
Love My Life

You Make Me
Love My Life

You Make Me
Love My Life

You Make Me
Love My Life

YOU CAN TRUST ME

You Can Trust Me
Though Others Fall Away
Don't Have A Doubt
I Will Be With You
When You're Dregged Out
I'll Be There Too
You Can Trust Me

I Don't Know Why
I Can't Seem To Cope
I Don't Know Why I Always Fall Away
Why Do I Turn My Back On Hope
I Am Useless For Today

You Can Trust Me
Though Others Fall Away
Don't Have A Doubt
I Will Be With You
When You're Dregged Out
I'll Be There Too
You Can Trust Me

Whatever You Say
I Believe
I Never Thought
You Would Ever Leave Me
If I Ever Lost My Way
It's Just So Hard Sometime
To Stay

You Can Trust Me
Though Others Fall Away
Don't Have A Doubt
I Will Be With You
When You're Dregged Out
I'll Be There Too
You Can Trust Me

WE WILL GO ON

Above You
Below Me
You're Standing
But It's Steep

I Love You
You Like Me
Our Time Is
Descending

But We Go On

Persistence
Don't Give Up
We'll Make It
We Will Go On

Above You
Below Me
We're Buried
Head Deep

I Love You
You Like Me
Our Time Is
Descending

But We Go On

Persistence
Don't Give Up
We'll Make It
We Will Go On

We Will Go On

We Will Go On

ANOTHER NEW DAY

Don't Throw
Your Life Away
Don't Give Up
You Will
Have Your Say
Yesterday
Is Not Today

Don't Make It
More Than It Is
Help Is Coming
Your Way
I'll Tell You
Like It Is
Now Put Some
Light On It

You Can Do
Wonders
Nobody Can
Hold You Back
But You
You Can Fly
In A Plane
And A Rocketship Too

You Have
Great Value
You Can't
Be Bought
Nor Sold
If You Lost Your Way

Tomorrow Is
Another New Day

Don't Throw Your Life Away
Don't Give Up
You Will Have Your Say
Yesterday Is Not Today

WHEN I LOOK INTO YOUR EYES

It Used To Be So Easy
When I Was Completely
Within My Own Senses
Then I Looked

Into Your Eyes

Now I'm In Trouble

When I Looked
Into Your Eyes
You Made Me Stumble

When I Looked
Into Your Eyes

I'm Sure You Get
A Lot Of Attention
From The Guys
That You Must Know
And Usually
I Handle My Disposition
But Now I Just Can't
Be That Wise

When I Looked
Into Your Eyes
Now I'm In
Trouble

When I Looked
Into Your Eyes
You Made Me Stumble

When I Looked
Into Your Eyes

I Am Defenseless
I Am So Uncool
I Lose My Senses
When I Look At You

When I Look
Into Your Eyes
I Am In
Trouble

When I Look
Into Your Eyes
You Make Me Stumble

When I Look
Into Your Eyes

THE ROAD

The Road We Put Our Feet To
Might Be An Uphill Climb
But When We Reach The Top Of
The Place Where God Stops Time

You And I
Will Be Together
Laughing At
Things We Used To Do
Seeing Everything
God Planned For Us
Before The Creation
Of The World

You And I

You'll Go And Ask Your Questions
And He'll Tell Us Everything
He'll Show Us How He Makes
And Measures The Stars
Flying Around Through Worlds
We Couldn't Know Before
Baby You Know We'll Go That Far

Its Easy To Let Our Troubles
Become More Than They Are
But When We Look At Heaven
The Troubles Seem So Small

You And I

You'll Go And Ask Your Questions
And He'll Tell Us Everything
He'll Show Us How He Makes
And Measures The Stars
Flying Around Through Worlds
We Couldn't Know Before
Baby You Know We'll Go That Far

NOT A GOOD MAN

I am Not A Good Man
I Tried Before But You Know How I Am
I Am Not A Good Friend
I'm Not The Kind You Keep Till The End

I Wanted You Forever
But Love Is A Two Way Street
I Know You Think Your Way Is Better
You Can Play Everyone You Meet

Don't Call Me
Don't Help Me
I Don't Want You
I Reject You
Go Away From Me
Go Away From Me

I am Nothing To You
I Thought You Were The One
To Give My Heart To
Now I Don't

I Have Nothing To Say
If You Wanted To Hear
Love Honor Obey
You Won't

I Wanted You Forever
But Love Is A Two Way Street
I Know You Think Your Way Is Better
You Can Play Everyone You Meet

Don't Call Me
Don't Help Me
I Don't Want You
I Reject You
Go Away From Me
Go Away From Me

I Can Be Much Better
Things Will Be Way Better
I Can Be Much Better
Things Will Be Way Better

LOVE ME TO THE GROUND

Take Your Light Out
And Throw It Into The Sea
Then The Waves
Will Bring Your Light To Me
Across The World
I'll Wait For You To Guide My Way
I Have No Doubt
Cause I Believe You Made This Day

Love Means Please Be Patient
Love Means Please Be Kind
Don't Hold My Wrongs
Against Me
Love Renews Your Mind

Love Means Do Not Envy
Love Is Never Proud
Love Is Always Hopeful
Love Me To The Ground

I'M FLYING HOME

I'm Flying Home
I Need You Close My Baby
Six AM Flight
My Bags Are Packed
I'm Waiting
Above The Clouds
Floating My Love To You

I'm Coming Home
Over The World
Godspeed Climbing
I'm Coming Home

I'm Flying Home
I'll Be There Soon I Promise
You Tell The Kids For Me
This Gig Is Almost Finished
Above The Clouds
Floating My Love To You

I'm Coming Home
Over The World
Godspeed Climbing
I'm Coming Home

I'm Coming Home
Over The World
Godspeed Climbing
I'm Coming Home

FROM YOUR OWN WORLD

I Don't Hope To Agree
With You My Love
Your Sadness Rolls Over Me
That I Can't Bring You Out Of

Could You Tell Me
Whatever Do You Want From Me
You Tell Me Something Strange Now
Aivd I Can't Possibly Agree
From Your Own World

I Don't Understand
Why You Let Them Take Your Life
The Existence Of Man
Is A Spirit Field Of Strife

Could You Tell Me
Whatever Do You Want From Me
You Tell Me Something Strange Now
And I Can't Possibly Agree
From Your Own World

Let's Leave Blame To The Devil
We Need That Space For Hope
When You Walk On Satan Avenue
You Need God Not You To Cope

Could You Tell Me
Whatever Do You Want From Me
You Tell Me Something Strange Now
And I Can't Possibly Agree
From Your Own World

CHAPTER 8

ETERNITY CALLED NOW

Where Have You Been Hiding
Mystery
Everything Has Been
Down Low
Soon As I Look Out
In Front Of Me
The Images Have Changed
Before I Know

This Whole World Is
All About The Twisting
In And Out Of
The End Is The Beginning
What Is Strange Now
Soon Will Be Forgotten
Spend Our Days In
Eternity Called Now

I had A Problem
With My Life Today
I Didn't Know
Why I Was Here

All These Happenings
Are Just Me Living Me
Struggles And Joy
I Feel So Near

This Whole World Is
All About The Twisting
In And Out Of
The End Is The Beginning
What Is Strange Now
Soon Will Be Forgotten
Spend Our Days In
Eternity Called Now

We Spend Our Days In This
Eternity Called Now

We Spend Our Days In This
Eternity Called Now

DEATH PARTY

Where Are The Lovely People
I Thought That I Would See
Diamonds And Smiles So Beautiful
But, That's Not Reality

Where Are Your Baby Girls Now
There's Something Wrong With This Scene
Whatever Did Mao Say To You
To Get You To Lose Your Chi

Whoever Said We'd All Live In Peace
Was Mistaken
If You Believe That We Will Evolve
Look Around You
Wake Up And See The Vision
Of Our Inhumanity
We're Not A Global Village
This World Is A Death Party

Where Are The Lovely People
I Saw On My TV
They Don't Get That Channel
In This Other World Country

Did God Tell You To Kill Me
Cause I Don't Believe In Him
How Is It Worship To Murder
Who's The Great Satan In Sin

Whoever Said We'd All Live In Peace
Was Mistaken
If You Believe That We Will Evolve
Look Around You
Wake Up See The Vision
Of Our Inhumanity
We're Not A Global Village
This World Is A
Death Party

MY BLACK HOUSE

In My Black House
Lives A Woman I Fear
Captive People Walking
But Not Out Of Here
My Straw Neck Binding
I Break Off
Hope The Secret Doorway
Is Wide Enough

Like A Radio
Tuned To Hell
That's Left On
I Can Not Seem
To Turn It Off

Out The Hidden Door
I See A Still Ocean
Black Bass On The Floor
With Bad Intonation
Eyes Do Not See
All That Is Around Them
They Don't See The War
That We All Fight In

You Look For Me
I Hide By The Passage
Then I Step Out Free
My Soul You Can't Damage
I Slap Your Hands Away
We Move In A Circle
As We Spin You Change
To You Way Younger

Like A Radio
Tuned To Hell
That's Left On
I Can Not Seem
To Turn It Off

FILTHY RICH

I'm Filthy Rich I Can Buy You
I've Got Big Bucks You Love Me
I'll Buy Your Momma And You'll Like It
I'll Take Your Spine You Smile

Mr. President I Own You
Judge For Rent I Bought You
This Legislature Makes Laws For Me
The Congressmen On Your TV

I'm Filthy Rich I Can Buy You
I Roll High Bucks You Love It
I'll Buy Your Momma That's A Fact
I Take Your Spine You Smile Back

I'll Take Your Daughter She's Seventeen
In My Private Jet You Worship Me
You Idolize Me Because I Can
Buy Your Life With A Swipe Of My Pen

I'm Filthy Rich I Can Buy You
I've Got Big Bucks You Love Me
I'll Buy Your Momma And You'll Like It
I'll Take Your Spine You Smile

If I Get Caught I Don't Worry
With My Best Friends Wife She Won't Whine
I've Got The Best Attornies
Make Him Run For His Life, They're Expensive Swine

If You Got Something I Want I'll Take It
I'm Powerful Don't Mind Killing You
Your Blood Won't Darken My Beautiful Day
My Money Speaks It Yells I'm Okay

I'm Filthy Rich I Can Buy You
I Roll High Bucks You Love It
I'll Buy Your Momma That's A Fact
I Take Your Spine You Smile Back

WHO AM I

I Am Leaving The Boundaries Of God's Order
The Laws Of Existence Here Are Not Normal
Circular Pulling From My Back Into Blackness
Blood Drawn Away From My Arms Into The Vortex

Who Am I
I Don't Know What Rovert Is
I Think He Is Three Different Things
Who Am I
A Vacuum Is Pulling Back My Head

My Body Is Pulled Away Into To A Formless Existence
Stripped Away In Windings Despite My Resistance
Coleen Stares Not Knowing, Karissa Speaks Reality
Can't Stop This Tangent Approaching Criticality

Who Am I
Who Is In Control Now
What Is Happening To My Life
Who Am I
As I'm Jumping Off This Life Plane

I Don't Sense God Here In This Demons Congregation
He Has Awareness Of All The Souls That Was My Last Assumption
I've Returned To This Place Of Continual Horror Manifestation
Thrust Into Eternal Life, I've Made A Grave Miscalculation

Who Am I
My Life Is Being Transferred
From Peace To Perpetual Fright
Who Am I
I Can't Hold On

Who Am I
I'm Whirling Toward Polarity
The Terror Waiting For Me
Who Am I
The Seeker Is Upon Me

Who Am I
Now Life Slowly Spirals Back In
Reversal Of Misfortune
I'm So Incredibly Thankful
But Who Am I

URANIUM DEMON

You Worry Me Baby
When You Sit There Like That
We May Not Ever
Find Our Way Back
I Put My Ear To The Ground
And Listen For Vibrations
Too Low To Be Heard
By The Satellite Rotations Round The World

You Brought Me Here
Though I Felt Uneasy
I Should Have Known
Not To Resist My Own Feelings
We Brought Down These People
But We Don't Have To Like It
Too Late For The Souls Separated
From Their Whole Lives

I Woke Up At Midnight
With The Sun In My Eyes
Numb And Astonished
That I Was Alive
And I Swore To Myself
And To God And To Man
Never To Conjure
That Uranium Demon Again

I Stand On The Shore
That Once Was A Great City
By Stinking Burned Bodies
That Once Were So Pretty
And Ask The Same Question
To My Troubled Brain
If Man Is Evolving
Why Is He
Increasing The Pain

SACRED HATRED

Oh God
Of This World
Pseudonym
Be Your Name
Your Kingdom
Will Come
Your Will
Will Be Done
On Earth
As It Is In Hell

Sacred Hatred

Give Us This Day
Our Daily Sins
And Remember
Our Trespasses
We Will Accuse Others
Who Trespass Against Us
Oh Ruler Of This World

Sacred Hatred

Lead Me
Into Temptation
And Deliver Me
Unto Evil
For Yours Is
This Kingdom
And Power
And Glory
For This Age
Amen

YESTERDAY YOU TOLD ME

Yesterday You Told Me
You Were Glad I Was Around
Yesterday You Told Me
You Were Glad To Have Me Around
Today You Want To Send Me
To The Lost And Found

I Was Proud When You Told Me
I Was Your Real Man
I Was Proud When You Told Me
I Was Your Real Man
Now You're Telling Secrets
To The Bassman In The Band

You Make It Look So Easy
To Play Me As A Fool
You Make It Look So Easy
To Play Me As A Fool
But I Won't Take It Anymore
You Broke The Golden Rule

You're Lying To Yourself
If You Think You're Not Alone
Girl You're Lying To Yourself
When You Think You're Not Alone

I'm Gonna Wake You Up
Early Tomorrow
And Send You
Back On Home

Yesterday You Told Me
You Were Glad I Was Around
Yesterday You Told Me
You Were Glad To Have Me Around
Today You Want To Send Me
To The Lost And Found

I ACT WELL, I'M REALLY EVIL

I Act Well
I'm Really Evil
I Won't Stop
Till I Get My Fill
Could You Ever
Pull The Plug On Me

Just Like Me
You're Innocent
Until You're Guilty
Outside You're Clean
But In You're Filthy
For What You've Done
You Sure Deserve To Die

Just Like You
I'm A
Sinner In My Mind
In The End
Every Night
I Murder My Friends
To Save Myself
I'll Grind You Into Meat

Yes
Who Who Hah

Who Who Hah Hah

Who Hah
Who Who
Hah Hah

Who Hah
Who Who
Hah Hah
Who

PLEASE DON'T WALK
AWAY FROM ME

Please Don't Walk
Away From Me
I Can't Chase You
On My Knees
Please Don't Walk
Away From Me
I Can't See Through These Tears
Baby Please

Please Don't Sweep
My Shoes Away
I Need To Put Them
On My Feet Today
And Find That Lady
From San Francisco Bay
Please Give Me My Shoes
And I'll Be On My Way

Please Don't Take Your
Love From Me
Give It Back Now
Baby Please
You Say I Don't Deserve You
Like I'm A Disease
After All These Years
I Do Agree

Please Don't Take
My World From Me
Don't Make Me Howl
Incessantly
Please Don't Take
My World From Me
Turn That Hate Into Love For Me
Baby Please

Please Don't Walk
Away From Me
I Can't Chase You
On My Knees
Please Don't Walk
Away From Me
I Can't See Through These Tears
Now Baby Please

THREE ARE THE PEOPLE

Why Don't You
Close Your Eyes
You've Got To
Trust Somebody
Listen To
Your Heart Cries
Not Your Money

One Is A Wonder
Two Make A Tune
Three Are The People
Forever You

To See Through
Life's Illusion
You Cannot
Be A Slave
Stay Out Of
The Confusion
Hate Is
An Early Grave

One Is A Wonder
Two Make A Tune
Three Are The People
Forever You

YOU MAY HAVE HEARD
ABOUT THE LORD

You May Have Heard About The Lord
And Thought He Was Just Someone's Dream
Or A Hopeful Wish Of The Downhearted
When I Met Him My Life Started

I Want To Tell You
My Life Is
Not The Same
God Really Loves You
I'm A Witness
Speaking In His Name
He Loves You

You Only Believe What You Touch See
You Want To Use Only Your Senses
Can You See Love Or Touch Hope In Me
You're Shut Out By Emotional Fences
Can You See?

You May Have Heard About The Lord
And Thought He Was Just Someone's Dream
Or A Hopeful Wish Of The Downhearted
When I Met Him My Life Started

I Want To Tell You
My Life Is
Not The Same
God Really Loves You
I'm A Witness
Speaking In His Name

He Loves You

GOD WITH US

You Are
God
With Us

You Told Us There Would
Be A Time
When We Would Worship
In Spirit And In Truth

They Saw The Light
Yet Then Chose The Darkness
And Man's Heart Would
Fail For Fear

And They Will Ask
The Mountains To Fall Upon Them
But The Mountains
Will Not

You Are
God
With Us

THE LORD IS GOOD

The Lord Is Good
He Will Answer You
He Made You And Me
And He Wants Us To Be Free

We Can Know
What He Thinks
By His Word
His Living Word

I Call You Friend
Sweet Child Of Mine
You Ask Me Why
Do I Care
For A Life
Caught Between Heaven And Hell

I Can Tell You
What You Mean To Me
With My Own Life

I Came To You And Offered Myself On A Cross
And Then I Died
So You Could Live

The Lord Is Good
He Loves You And Me
And His Love And His Grace
And His Mercy Endure
For All Time
For Every Time

You Ask Me Why Is He Good
How Does He Know

I Can Only Tell You
What I See In My Own Life
I Once Did Not Know How
To Get Out Of My Pain

And Then I Died
And Birthed A Gain

The Lord Is Good

GOD AND I

God And I
Can Do Anything
In This Universe
We Can Role Over The Ocean
On A Skinny Nurse

She'll Say That We
Quenched Her Thirst
He's The Last
And He's The First

God And I
Don't Sweat
Even The Really Really Big Stuff

And He's In Control Of Everything
You Even Haven't Thought Of
His Spirit Comes As A Dove
My Dad Is The God Of Love

God And I

God And I

CHAPTER 9

GIANTS

Four Giants All Around Me
I'm Trying To Avert A Tragedy
If I Can Make It Through These Trees
I Would Never Leave My Family

And I Hear You Walking
So Close To Me
I Hold In My Breath Tightly
In This Emergency

My Ears Don't Stand Up Straight
But I Can Hear Very Well
I Keep The Giants Up At Night
In My Paranoid Guarding Hell

And I Hear You Walking
So Close To Me
I Hold In My Breath Tightly
In This Emergency

Four Giants All Around Me

Four Giants All Around Me

GOODBYE TO WONDERING

Goodbye To Wondering
Truth Stands Still Before You
You Have A Right To Disbelieve
All The Way To Hell

Would God Come To Your Relief
If You Could Do It On Your Own
How Many Times Can You Hear The Call
Before Your Heart Says Come On Home

Your Mind Is A Battle Raging
And Lies Are Your Trusted Friends
Your Eyes See Only When You're Crying
Your Soul Stays Alive When You're Dead

Could So Many Answers Be
The Way To The Only God
He Already Gave You The Key
Why Then Do You Still Search On

Don't Look To Man For What You Need
Tears Will Follow Endlessly
Pride And Lies Grow Bountifully
You Need The Breath Of God To See

Lay Down Your Needs One By One
Till There's Nothing Near Or Far
Get Free Of The Façade Of Self
Find Out Who You Really Are

Find A New Thing In Your Heart
That Was Always There Before
You Can Find It Only When
You Realize Your Own Despair

FAILING MY WAY TO YOU

Watching For The Time
When My Life Jumps Over The Line
Waiting For The Light
To Take Me Where I Know Is Mine

Standing On The Edge
Of The Place That Looks Out
Over Time
Wondering Out Loud
How Do I Move From Hell
To Sublime

Pointing The Way To You
Nightmares Are Coming True
Failing My Way To You
Please Help Me Make It Through

People Follow You
Killing Everyone
Who Doesn't Agree
Calling On Your Name
As They Disobey Your Decree

It's Not Hard To See That Lies
Have Fooled Them All
Man's Hate For His Brother
And Satan Make Them Fall

Watching For The Time
When My Life Jumps Over The Line
Waiting For The Light
To Take Me Where I Know Is Mine

INTO REAL LIFE

I Can See You've Gone
From Dark To Light
I Can Feel Your Spirit
Left The Night

Did You Thank God
For Saving You
Holy Spirit
Now Is Driving You

God Is Not A Man
That He Should Lie
We'll All Be Together
Up On High

God And Angels
Are Rejoicing On You
Now Your Heart
Is Flowing With The Truth

A New Person Is
Born Again Today
Into Real Life

TO BE FREE

You've Got TheWind
At Your Back Today
Above The Clouds
You Know The Way
Touching Heaven
Not Lost In Yourself Now
He Spoke Truth
When He Told You How

To Be Free
To Be Free
He Set Us Free

He Wouldn't Lie To You
He Wouldn't Sweat Blood
For Something To Do

The Veil Ripped For You
Jesus Loved You
Before You Knew

There's No Other Name Under Heaven
Upon Which Man Is Saved
There's No One Like Messiah
Gave His Life For You And Me

To Be Free
To Be Free
He Set Us Free

He Wouldn't Lie To You
He Wouldn't Sweat Blood
For Something To Do
The Veil Ripped For You
Jesus Loved You Before You Knew

HOLD ON TO THE LOVE

You Took My Love
Then You Walked On Bye
The Only One
To Make Me Feel Alive

I Guess You Just Don't Understand
How It Feels To Lose Your Heart

Emotions Fray When They Bend Too Far
M.I.A. In The Family War
I Try To Stop The Pain Inside
I Gotta Learn To Live My Own Life

Hold On To The Love

Just Follow The Love
That You Find In The River
The River Of Living Water
Jump Off With Both Feet
You Will Land In The Middle
Go And Tell Everyone You Meet

All Your Days
You Know Are Numbered
All That Time
Already Spent
Come Out Of Your Hiding Place
Everyone Is Waiting For You

They Tell You Time
Will Take You Under
You Know Too Well
All That They Meant

You Never Lost Your Soul Inside
You Just Need To Find The New Life

Hold On To The Love

C'mon And Follow The Love
That You Find In The River
The River Of Living Water
Jump Off With Both Feet
You Will Land In The Middle
Go And Tell Everyone You Meet

DON'T CRY

Everybody Is Trying To Play The Game
But That Doesn't Have To Leave You In The Pain
If You Know The Reason Why You Came
Does It Matter If Your Cousin Doesn't Feel The Same

Don't Cry
Don't Cry

You've Only Seen The Winter
It's Not The Only Season
Come Out And Feel The Wonder
It's Not Too Late

Don't Cry
Don't Cry

I Wouldn't Want To Drive With You In Your Car
You Might See The Demon Who Made You Who You Are
There's Nothing Really Wrong With You
That Couldn't Be Improved With A New Change Of View

Don't Cry
Don't Cry

You've Only Seen The Winter
It's Not The Only Season
Come Out And Feel The Wonder
It's Not Too Late

Don't Cry
Don't Cry

Don't Cry
Don't Cry

WHERE IS YOUR LOVE

You Obey All The Rules
You Judge Yourself Highly
When Your Brother Falls
Your Hand Points Slyly

Where Is The Love
Show Me Let Me See It

Where Is Your Love
Come On Make Me Feel It

You've Got Your Nose In Your Money
But You're Bankrupt In Love
What You Do Have Is Empty
Concealed From Above

Where Is The Love
Show Me Let Me See It

Where Is Your Love
Come On Make Me Feel It

Where Is The Love
Show Me Let Me See It

Where Is Your Love
Come On Make Me Feel It

DERANGED

I Really Wouldn't Want To Love You
Any More Than I Do Now
I Think That Would Be Dangerous
For Everyone Involved

You Said That Someday We
Could Take Some Time Before We Part
You Can Take My Ligament
And I Could Have Your Heart

Glue My Soul Down I'm About To Be Undone
Take Me Out Of This Give Me A Chance To Run
Believe Me I Am Not The One
You Don't Believe Me

So Many Times I've Looked Up
Into Your Deep Black Ceiling
And Want To Say The Ugly Evil Things
That I Have Been Feeling

But I Can't Say That To You
With This Mask Upon My Face
I Never Wanted To Be A Part Of Your
Unholy Human Race

Glue My Soul Down I'm About To Be Undone
Take Me Out Of This Give Me A Chance To Run
Believe Me I Am Not The One
You Don't Believe Me

I Love You
I Live You
I Don't Think We Should Do This Anymore

PO, SAD AND UGLY

Maybe I Could Play
A Song For You
Maybe You'll Think
That I'm So Cool
Or Maybe
You're Feeling Lonely
And You Don't Care
If I'm A Fool

Maybe I Could Impress You
With My Might
Make Your Troubles
Dissolve Into The Night
Maybe You'll See Me
As Your Friend
I'd Walk All The Way On My Hands
To See You Just Once Again

You Said
I'm Po, Sad And Ugly
I Cannot Help
Two Of The Three
I'm Po, Sad And Ugly
If You Can't Love Me
Just Let Me Be

I Asked You If You Liked My Song
You Told Me That I Just Don't Belong
You Think I Would Know All This By Now
I've Heard The Words Before You Said Some How

I Know The Stars Would Bring Us Romance
If You Would Just Give Me One Chance
But You Look At Me With All Disdain
Why Do You Constrain Me In This Pain

You Say
I'm Po, Sad And Ugly
I Cannot Help
Two Of The Three
I'm Po, Sad And Ugly
If You Can't Love Me
Just Let Me Be

ON THE MINDWAY

Why Do A Thousand People Die
When They Look So Bright And Shiny
Love Is Swallowed Up By Hate
And You Ride So High And Mighty

Standing On The Wedding Cake
Dressed Up Now But Soon You're Weeping
Fingers Read The Actors Face
Dirty Gold Is Not Worth Keeping

Tell Me
Are You There
On The Mindway

Watch The Fools Give Your Life Away
While You Eat Your TV Dinner
In The Winter You Are Walking
Old Dogs And The Mice Are Thinner

Wonder If You Can Remember
Your Enemy Is Now Your Neighbor
There Must Be Some More To This
Living All Your Life In Danger

Tell Me
Are You There
On The Mindway

WATERLADY

I Don't Know
How To Speak
I Only Memorize You See
I Cannot Even Read
My Fortune Tea

I Try To Just Fit In
I Wear The Clothes
My Neighbor Has
I Hope I Don't Offend
My Waterlady

She Just Put Out
My Cigarette
Told Me Not To
Stand Still
I Can't Hear
Cause My Ears Are Wet
I Need A Life Preserver

My Car Is Ill Equipped
It Comes With Underdrive
My Killer Bees Are Using
Me For A Hive

The Brothers Tell Me I
Burned Up My Autojive
I Need The Waterlady To Survive

She Just Put Out
My Cigarette
Told Me Not To
Stand Still
I Can't Hear
Cause My Ears Are Wet
I Need A Life Preserver

She Just Put Out
My Cigarette

She Just Put Out
My Cigarette

LAST COMPLEX

I've Got So Many Things To Do
So Get Out Of My Way You Pest
I've Got Not Time Enough For You
So Don't You Block My Progress

I've Got No Time For Myself
I Need A Year Vacation
But I'm Making All This Cash
I'll Buy Sleep Medication

I've Got Little Time On My Hands
And So Much I Should Be Doing
I've Got Forty People Who Need Me
Away I'll Send Them Turning

If I Had A Reason To Care
I Might Try To Change Something
I've Got Nothing Else To Give Myself
Life Is So Frustrating

I've Got Too Little Time To Think
And So Much That Needs Re-thinking
If My Reasoning Would Not Hide
I Could Keep Myself From Sinking

I Feel Too Much Pressure On Me
So Don't Get Too Close To Me
My Chest Hurts I Can't Breathe
A New Heart Is What I Do Need

I've Had Way Too Much Extreme
I Need Someone To Help Me
There's No Sleeping Through This Dream
That Wakes Me Up So Early

Now I'm Wondering If It's True
There's No Reason For All These Blues
I Can't Trust All Of My Thoughts
Because Some Are From Me And Some Are From You

WITCH

You Don't Know What It Is
That I Have Against You
Maybe It's The Thing
About The Potions And Blood
I Think That We Should
Both See Other People
I Really Miss
That Little Trait Called Love

I Don't Want To Worship A Goddess
I Don't Like The Sacrifice
I Don't Even Own A Black Candle
Don't Want To Drink Blood At Night

My Friends Say You Look Like A Devil
You Take That As A Compliment
In Time You'll Earn A Medal
But Could You Leave
Before My Life Is Too Bent

I Don't Want To Worship Your Goddess
I Don't Like The Sacrifice
I Don't Even Own A Black Candle
Don't Want To Drink Blood At Night

I Don't Know
Why It Bothers My Conscience
You Always Tell Me
You're Are A Good Witch
But In Cold Sweat I Wake Up
Every Night Since
I Found Your Dagger
And The Skulls In The Ditch

I Don't Want To Worship Your Goddess
I Don't Like The Sacrifice
I Don't Even Own A Black Candle
Don't Want To Drink Blood At Night

WHY I WONDER

So Many Years Of Fighting
And We're Both On The Wrong Side
I Can't See My People
Cause They're Out On The Run

Never In Our Lifetime
Will We See What You're After
I'm Sure I'm Not The Only One
Who's Not Having Fun

Why, Why I Wonder
Why, Don't You Wonder

Launching Missiles At Cities
Hoping We Will Not See Them

Look At The People We Lost
I Guess You No Longer Need Them

Ten Ton Explosion
No Loss Of Emotion

I Think We Better Move Underground

Around The World In Silence
Don't Look At The Violence
I Guess I Just Don't See That Evolution

Ambivalent Injustice
You're Trying To Disgust Us
Can't We Have A World
Where We Can Live And Not Run

I Think I Will Not Believe Them
You Better Not Believe Them

CHAPTER 10

HOUSE OF MISREPRESENTATIVES

Blood Was Shed
For The Union
We Could Work And Thrive

Now Our Government
Rapes The System
Middle Class Suicide

The Rich Won't Keep Them Out
Improves Their Bottom Line

Politicians Turn Their Faces
Got To Keep On Winning Races
You Can Speak With Your Vote
Put Some Feet On Your Hope

Or Maybe It's Time To Give Up Just Hoping

I Was A Union Man
From The Shrinking Middle Class
Lost My Home And My Land
My Wife Just Could Not Last

We Sat And Watched Our Children Leave
They Couldn't Find A Job To Succeed
They Need A Fighting Chance
Can You Hear Them Sighing

Who Can Restore Their Faith

Congress Stopped Representing
The Electorate Long Ago
Those We Pay For Consenting
Legislate For Money And Ego

I Was A Union Man
From The Shrinking Middle Class
Lost My Home And My Land
My Wife Just Could Not Last

CRAZIES FROM THE STREET

The Crazies From The Street
The People I Just Love To Meet
Are All Here Tonight
For Some Food And Sleep And Blight
Most Do Not Notice My Entry
Or The Stale Urine Scent Of The Rabid Gentry

Take Me Away
From This Place Lord
I Don't Want To Be Here
Take Me Next Door
Take Me Away

Gray Beard Skinny With Furtive Una Bomber Glances
Alkies And Junkies Lost In Their Own Trances
Backpack Cruiser Looking At His Toes
Poking For Brain Finger In His Nose
Encroaching Pain Is Sloughing
Endemic Is The Deep Lung Coughing

Take Me Away
From This Place Lord
I Don't Want To Be Here
Take Me Next Door
Take Me Away

The Old Queen Gives Her Bible Away
To A Monk Wearing One Sandal And A Sneaker For Play
Weird Wig On The Friday Preacher
Talks About God But The People Are The Feature
Till My Senses Lead Me Out Into The Night
Outside The Door Into The Railroad Fight

Wash My Clothes Wash My Hair
Wash My Feet I Don't Care
Close The Door I Don't Wanna Eat
Hide Me From The People That Come From The Street

Take Me Away
From This Place Lord
I Don't Want To Be Here
Take Me Next Door
Take Me Away

LOVE WITH ME

Long Legs
Blue Couch Eyes
Skinny Lips
Skinny Hips

Ooh I Love To Love You Baby
Ooh I Love To Love You Baby

I Don't Know All
About True Love
I Don't Know
About The Stars Above
I Need Only Two Things In My Life
One Is The Lord
And The Other Is My Wife

Ooh I Love To Love You Baby
Ooh I Love To Love You Baby

I Never Wanted To Live Forever
I Never Wished That I'd Be Free
I Only Wanted To Find Another
One Who Could Love With Me

Ooh I Love To Love You Baby
Ooh I Love To Love You Baby

THIS STRANGE FATE

There's Something
I Did Not Tell You
I Contracted Something
Before I Met You

I Would Never
Try To Harm You
I Really Love You
Didn't Want To Lose You

I Really Love You

Why Would You Not Even
Tell That To Me
You Would Have Taken
My Choice To Be Free
Why Would You Take
The Risk Of My Life To Be
I Thought That Love Meant
You Cared About Me

I Guess I Should Have
Told You About
The Mistakes I Made
That Tear My Heart Out

Now I'm Lost
In This Strange Fate
But There's Still A Chance For You
If It's Not To Late

MORE THAN YOU GOT

There Are Many Roads To God You Said
You Chose The Wider One To Walk On
If You Spend Your Life Wondering
Who Will Redeem You When You're Dead

Living Your Life That Way
In Darkness Night Is The Day

Tell Me Why You Do It
I Couldn't Go Through It

Sometimes It Takes More Than You Got
Tears Are Flowing They Don't Stop
I Know Your Wounds Take Time To Bleed
Will You Ever Get What You Need

It's Hard To Believe That You Mean What You Say
I See Through Your Deception
Do You Remember When God Led Your Way
I Guess You Forgot To Mention

Living Your Life That Way
In Darkness Night Is The Day
Tell Me Why You Do It
I Couldn't Go Through It

Sometimes It Takes More Than You Got
Tears Are Flowing They Don't Stop
I Know Your Wounds Take Time To Bleed
Will You Ever Get What You Need

LUNATIC REASON

Your Lucky Number
The Sign You're Under
And The Charm You Use So Well
Should'nt You Know It All By Now

Your Sinister Plan
Scared Yes Men Follow You
Your Ministerial Pursuit
Is It You Who Has To Turn

Lunatic Reason
Lunatic Reason
Makes Only Teardrops
Pound As Thunder

You Say They're Just People
Stay Away From Me
With Your Sadistic Reality
Everyone Is A Person
Not Like You

Another New Day
Change Is Offered You
But You Live Your Lif'e The Same Way
Would It Hurt You To Find The Truth

You Turn A Deaf Ear
And Wink A Blind Eye
As Your People Hide In Fear
Can You Hear The Oppressed Cry

Lunatic Reason
Lunatic Reason
Makes Only Teardrops
Pound As Thunder

You Say They're Just People
Stay Away From Me
With Your Sadistic Reality
Everyone Is A Person
Not Like You

ONE PEOPLE

You Say You Got Nobody To Love
Shoulder To Your Enemy
You'll Shoot Him To The Stars Above
No Concept Of Your Family

You Look To The Creation For Strength
Grasping At The Things You Feel
The Fog From The Drugs You Take
Spins You Round An Endless Wheel

The Sand The Stars And The, Dust
The People Of The World You See
You Say It's Them Not Us
Hate Is Your Biography

People
One People
In The World
God Help Us

How Much Can You Really Take
How Long Can You Fake That Smile
Don't Count On The Money You Make
You Can't Buy A Life With Guile

Your Heart Is A Closed Dark Book
That You Let Nobody Read
When You Open Up And Look
Black Pages Fall On Me

The Sand The Stars And The, Dust
The People Of The World You See
You Say It's Them Not Us
Hate Is Your Biography

People
One People
In The World
God Help Us

I WANT YOU TO LOVE

I Would Spend Forever
Waiting For You
I Would Buy My Life
And Give It To You

I Want You
To Love

You Are Not A Figment
Of Some Insanity
But When I Try To Touch You
You Fade Away From Me
Don't Hide And Make Me Seek
I Need Your Love To Save Me

Take The Blood From My Veins
And Spill It Down The River
If I Cant Hold You In My Arms
There Is Nothing To Consider

I Want You
To Love

You Are Not A Figment
Of Some Insanity
But When I Try To Touch You
You Fade Away From Me
Don't Hide And Make Me Seek
I Need Your Love To Save Me

I LOVE MYSELF

I Love Myself
But I Don't Love Other People
I Don't Care If They All
Jump Off A Steeple
I May Talk To You Because
I Want Something From You
Maybe Your Love If I
Think It Will Do

Yeah
Me

I Love Myself
But I Hate Other People
I Married You Just For
What You Would Do For Me

We Have Two Fine Kids
For Our Good Pleasure
I Need To Love Me
Before I Can Love Another

I Love Myself
So You Better Take Heed
Stay Away From
Everything That I I Need

Don't Drive By Me
Stay Away, No Apology
I Love Just Me
Thanks To Modern Psychology

IT'S HAZARDOUS
TO LIVE IN THIS WORLD

It's Hazardous To Live In This World
Without A J. O. B.
All The People That You See
Are Slaves To The Economy

It's Hazardous To Be Alive
Change Your Nation To Survive
With A Number On Your Head
You Don't Choose, You Are Lead

Peace Is So Far Away

Wait A Little While
You'll See
Everything In This World
Is The Way It Has To Be
Let Me See You Smile
You Are Alive

It's Dangerous To Be Alive
With All The People That You Meet
Some Are Filled With Disease
Out Of Mouths Come Only Lies

This Oil Has Turned Red
The Bombs Have Made The Rebels Loyal
Did You Trust The Things They Said
Ten Piece Suit And Lying Smile

Peace Is So Far Away

Wait A Little While
You'll See
Everything In This World
Is The Way It Has To Be
Let Me See You Smile
You Are Alive

LIFE THAT'S SO PROFANE

Your Eyelids Are Heavy
Like Clouds About To Rain
Sorry To Disturb You
To Cause You So Much Pain

I Meant To Hurt You
I Know What I Have Done
Love Can Be So Brutal
Emotions On The Run

You Rise And I Fall
Listen To My Simple Call
Life Always Moves Too Fast
Last Will Be First, First Is Last

Hurts Me
Your Discontent
The Emotional Pain I Gave
Is Mine
You Are
So Innocent
Kills My Heart
Every Time

Happiness Not Realized
No Rejection Of My Pain
Keeps Me Desensitized
In This Life That's So Profane

THIS IS NOT HAPPENING

I Had A Nervous Mind
Wondering What To Do
You See It
Worked Out Fine
I Did Not See You

Through The Fires
And The Cauldrons
We Will Come Out Flying

This Is Killing Me
You Love Me
See You In Heaven
Fun Fun Fun

Through The Fires
And The Cauldrons
We Will Come Out Flying

This Is Not Happening
I Lost Myself
I Came Back Different
I Need Your Help

Through The Fires
And The Cauldrons
We Will Come Out Flying

HOLD THE FIRE

It Is Good To Be In This World
All The People You Can See
Don't Take Counsel From Fear
Who You Are Just Be

And You Can Live That Way
And You Will Understand
You Can Take The Weight
It's All In His Plan

As We Spin Round The World
And As We Fly Around The Sun
Would You Hold Back The Fire
If We Love Everyone

If Your Head Is In The Clouds
You Can Watch The Rain Falling Down
If Your Feet Touch The Ground
You Can Walk As One With The Crowd

Find The Good In This World

Would You

Would You

As We Spin Round The World
And As We Fly Around The Sun
Would You Hold Back The Fire
If We Love Everyone

Would You

CHANGE IN THE WORLD

A Mortally Wounded Man Will Be Healed
He Will Make Peace Throughout The Whole World
How Odd
He'll Be On Channel Seven News In The Field
He'll Be A Hero
You'll Call Him God

There Will Be A Change In The World
The Antichrist Is Coming
A Man Of Awesome Power
Miracles Fool The Children

On Hand Or Forehead Take The Mark
Six Six Six The Sign Of Man
Or Stand Before The Sword In The Dark
And Fight The War At Hand

There Will Be A Change In The World
There Will Be A Change In America
There Will Be A Change In The World

ARE YOU NOT IN THE WORLD

You Made The Wind
But You Are Not In The Wind
You Made The Earthquake
You Are Not In The Earthquake
You Made The Fire
But You Are Not In The Fire
You Created The World
Are You Not In The World

Go Stand On The Mountain
But Hide Your Face
Ask Your Question
If You Can Listen
He Has Left Some
Who Have Not Bowed Down
To The World
To The Ground

Your Voice Is Thunder
Your Voice Is Still And Small
Makes Us Wonder
How We Ever
Hear You At All
You Made The Sky
But You Are Not In The Sky
You Made Man
Are You Not In Man

WINTER SUN

At This Time Each Year
The Sun Slowly Begins To Thrust
It's Most Radiant And Beautiful Beams
Of Glowing Energy
Through Narrow And Cold Passageways

It Starts Also To Thaw This
Hardened Glacier I Most Reluctantly
Claim As My Own Heart

With Objectives Avowed
I Follow The Constricted Pathway North
Not Of Geographical Context
But Of Celestial Bearing

Above Dense Purple Clouds
That Peer Over The Temporal
There Exists A Plane Unlike Our Earthly Abode
Impervious To Human Frailty

In The Vacuum Of Desolation
Stolen Slivers Of Delusion
Fail To Incite A Modicum Of Hope
On This Pathway Of Devout Contrition

You Who Have Heard The Cry
Not Alone Will You Fend This Jagged Land
Against Our Nefarious And Astute Adversary
Still We Will Never Give Up
No Not Ever

To Permit A Spirit Of Fear
Is As Losing One's Life In This Realm
Light Is Lost In The Battle Of The Spirit

Scant Is The Road We See
But Another We Surely Will Not Follow

Those Who Fail Are Not Blamed
Or Thought As Foe
As Men They Wage Spiritual War
Bearing Mortal Weapons

We Won't Stop To Think
How Life Might Have Been
We Drink From The Cup That We Are Given

On A Measure Of Faith And Hope
In The Land Of The Spirit Without End
Floundering Forward
Through The Winter Sun
We Will Go

WHEN CAN I FLY

So Much Pain That I Live In
What Am I Supposed To Do
People I'm With Choose Sin
They Need To Get A Life
I Got One From You

Working Everyday Is A Struggle
Where Virtue Is Superfluous
I Can't Stay Here In This Morbid Bubble
How Can I Live In This Circus

When Can I Fly
Away From This Chaos
To A Better Place
Where You Can See Us
And Love Is On Your Face

Away From This Evil
That Injures My Heart
It's A Raw Deal
So Give Me A New Start
I Don't Wanna Die, But
When Can I Fly

The Top Is Definitely Upside Down
The World Is A Dangerous Place
When I Fall Up I Hit The Ground
Please NASA Send Me Into Space

Looks Like I'll Wait
My Seventy-Four Years
Till My Mind Is Gone
And My Body Is Ailing
Before I Hear
My Own Silent Cheers
When I Know
My Heart Is Finally Failing

Then I Can Fly

DO YOU SEE AT ALL

Five-Thousand People
With Just Two Fishes
And Your Water
Tastes Like Wine
Pharisees Are Talking
Lots Of Money
I Could See
But Now I'm Blind

All Over
The People Are Talking
About The Things
You Do
I'd Like To
Sell Some Healings
Make You Rich
And Me Too

If You're The Son Of God
Do You Know
I'm Lost

I Saw You When
The Wind Was Blowing
You Calmed Down The Storm
You Spoke To Lazarus That Morning
Let Him Come Back Home

Why Do You
Look At Me That Way
I Don't Want To Fall
Something In Your Eyes Today
You Know I'm Gonna Call
They're Waiting
Till The Light Goes Down
Out Behind The Wall
Why Do You Need To Wash My Feet
Do You See It All

THERE IS A MAN

There Is A Man
With Lightening In His Wings
Looked Up To See
The Sky Was Opening

There Is A Man
People Flocked To His Sleeve
He Scolded His Friend
Because He Did Not Believe

Throw Yourself Into The Sea
Self Is Not The Love
You Were Made To Be
Throw Yourself In The Sea
You're A Detriment To Humanity

There Is A Man
Read His Biography
You Need To Know Him
He Made You And Me

There Is A Man
He's Calling You To Life
Waiting For You
When Are You Going To Say Alright

Throw Yourself Into The Sea
Self Is Not The Love
You Were Made To Be
Throw Yourself In The Sea
You're A Detriment To Humanity

GOD'S GAME

In God's Game
We Are All Players
And If You Don't Know The Rules
You'll End Up A Loser

In God's Game
You Might Try To Cheat Your Way Through
Or Use Other Players
That Makes Them Play Against You

And God's Game Never Ends
But You Lose Your Place At The Table
Till The White Throne Judgment
Then You Want To Play Again
But You're Not Able

In God's Game
You Wake Up In A Movie
With No End And No Start
And If You Listen To The Director
He'll Give You The Best Part

In God's Game
That Movie Is Never A Rerun
But In Time The Credits Roll
Then You've Got To Pay Your Toll

And God's Game Never Ends
But You Lose Your Place At The Table
Till The White Throne Judgment
Then You Want To Play Again
But You're Not Able

POWERS YOU DO NOT SEE

Got A Line Got A Line On Me
In Your Book I'm Already There
Spend Some Time Today For Someone
Who Does Not Think Life Is Fair

I Know Somebody Is Out There
Thinking That They Took A Ride
From Someone Somewhere
And Got On The Far Side Of Hell

There Is A White Sphere
Its Truth And Light Are Pure
Born In Corruption
You Cannot See Or Hear

Darkness Blocks Your Thoughts
You Can't Trust What You Think
Mistakes Happen To Be Your Reality

The Devil Is The Father Of Lies
The Truth Is Not His Strategy
People Standing In Line
To Be The Next Sad Prodigy

Don't Mistake His Lies
For Your Reality
He's In Your World Now
He's Still In Your Good Company

Walking Down On The Street
You Bump Into A Principality
You Can See In Their Eyes
They Are Living In Insanity

Maybe That Person Is You Or Me
It's Hard To Hit
When You're Fighting
Powers You Do Not See

I WOULD GIVE MY WHOLE LIFE TO YOU

Would He Give His Whole Life To You
Would He Give His Last Breath For You
Would He Give The World That He Knows
Would He Give Everything He Holds

I Would Give My Whole Life To You

I Would Sow My Soul To Keep You
I Would Gladly Give My Heart To Reap You
I Would Never Lie Or Hurt You
I Would Rather Die Than Lose You

I Would Give My Whole Life For You

Honey If You Ever Need Me
I Would Stop The World From Moving
Baby I Would Live To Kiss You
Plan My Days And Nights To Never Miss You

I Would Give My Whole Life To You

Does He Count Each Minute When You're Gone
Does He Notice Everything You've Touched Or Done
Would He Give His Life To Have You
And Never Put Himself Before You

I Would Give My Whole Life For You

Would He Give You All That You Need
Would He Fight For You Until He Bleeds
I Think Of You A Thousand Times Each Day
Hoping Just Once You'll Think Of Me Some Way

I Would Give My Whole Life To You

I Would Give My Whole Life For You

I TRIED

I Tried To Be There On Time
I Tried To Show You Two Times
I Tried To Tell You Three Times
You Didn't Listen To Me

You Said You Didn't Agree
You Said You Didn't Need Me
Now You're Trying To Find The Things
You Said You Never Needed

I Could Tell You Bout The Things That I Believe In
I Could Bore You, Leave You Yawning In The Evening
I Could Show You How I Feel If You Want To
But That's Not Gonna Make You Feel
The Things The Way That I Do

I Tried To Be There On Time
I Tried To Show You Two Times
I Tried To Tell You Three Times
You Didn't Listen To Me

You Said You Didn't Agree
You Said You Didn't Need Me
Now You're Trying To Find The Things
You Said You Never Needed

Who Can Ever Really Know Another Soul Right
I Don't Even See The Sun And Know That It Is Starlight
Love To You Is Just Something That You Can't Find
Really Tell Me Baby Now, Don't You Have It In Your Mind

I Am Just One Single Life You Say I Am Wasting
Maybe One Day You Can Show Me How To Taste It
I Don't Need Your Hate, I Don't Need Your Confrontation
If I Were A God, I Couldn't Meet Your Expectation

I Tried To Be There On Time
I Tried To Show You Two Times
I Tried To Tell You Three Times
You Didn't Listen To Me

You Said You Didn't Agree
You Said You Didn't Need Me
Now You're Trying To Find The Things
You Said You Never Needed

MY MOM

You Were The Only Girl
In Your Daddy's Eyes
You Sang For Drunks
In Your Family's Restaurant
You Got A Job
When You Were Only Twelve
In The Depression
That Money Helped A Lot

You Married Two Men
One Was A Gentleman
One Was A Dope Fiend
And You Had Four Kids
Loved Us All As
Only A Mother Could
Made Up For All The Things
Our Father Did

You Walked With Hurt Feet
And Carried Groceries
It Was Painful For You But
We Own Those Memories
You Worked At Christmas
And You Traveled By Bus
To Make Some Extra Money
To Provide For Us

Now The Book Has Closed
Upon Your Life
But The Movie
Plays Back Every Hour
In All The Hearts Of Those
Who Knew Your Soul
A Seed Of Beauty
Grows A Wondrous Flower

NOW THAT YOU'RE AWAY

Maybe It's My Fault For
Letting You Near

I Did Not Think One Night Would
Lead Us To Here

Doesn't Make A Difference
Now That I'm Away

I Told You Don't Call Me
From That Old Dive
I Gave You A Present
I Let You Stay A Live

Doesn't Make A Difference
Now That I'm Away

Down In Dark Water They
Search For You There
No Trace, Did I Leave
Not That I Care

Doesn't Make A Difference
Now That You're Away

KILL PEOPLE

Kill People
The Pregnant Woman
Walking Down On The Street
Kill People
Take Out A Priest
Or A Cop On The Beat
Kill People
Off A Baby
With Her Dolls And Toy Combs
Kill People
Kill Everyone Asleep
In Safe Little Homes

Why Do Christians
Oppose Me And Say
Love One Another
You Were Born To Love Not Hate
Love Even Your Enemy
Loving Is Great

I Don't See What They Want
But I Know What They Need

Kill People
When They're Richer Than You
Kill People
If They Don't Look Like You
Kill People
When They Get In Your Way

Kill People
Get Some Every Day

K, I, L, L
Everybody Go To Hell

I Know You Want To
I Think You Want To
I Guess That You Want To

Do You Want To?